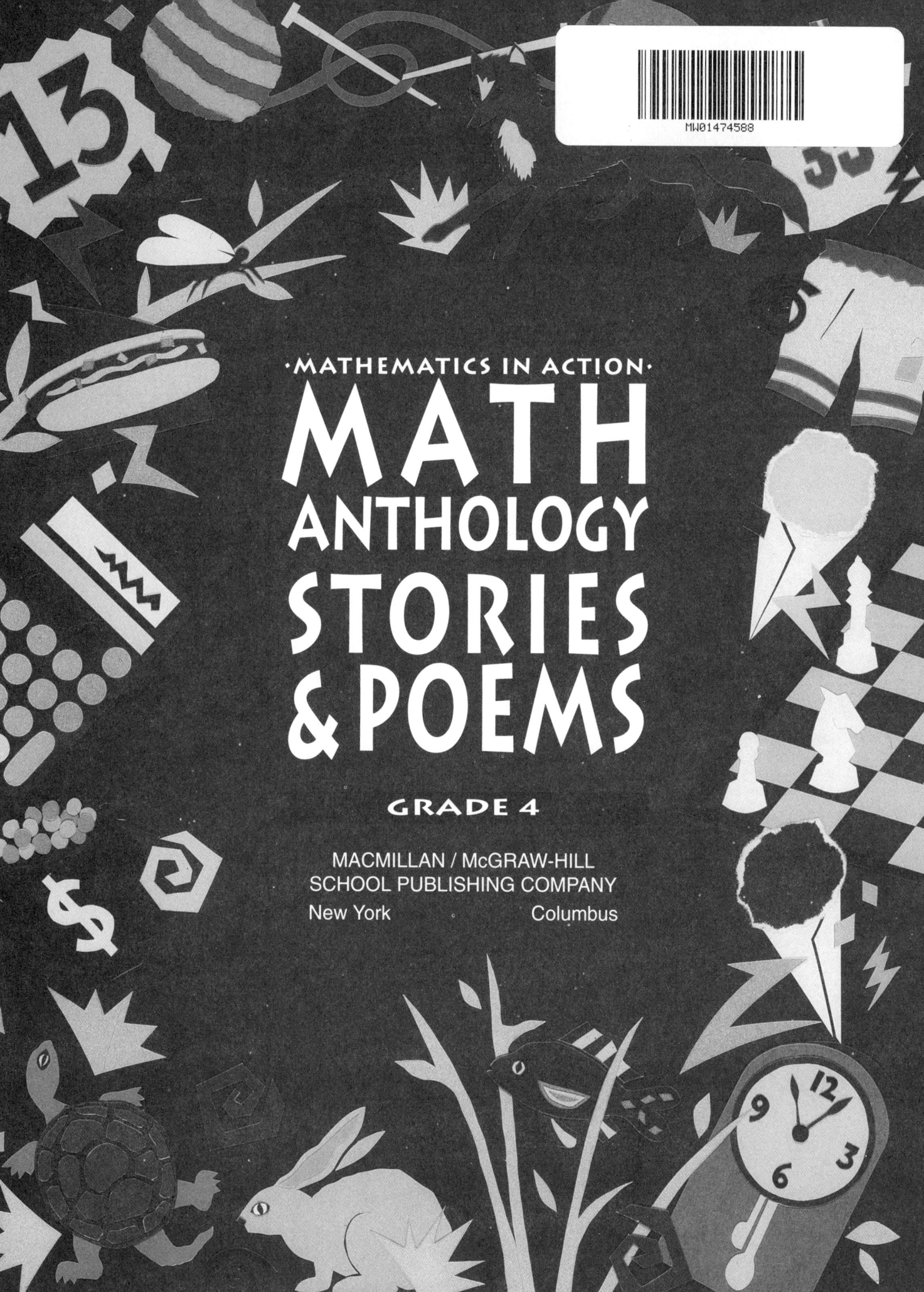

The **MATH ANTHOLOGY Stories and Poems** offers a variety of traditional and contemporary selections of children's literature. These selections are used as the basis for many of the individual and small-group activities in **MATHEMATICS IN ACTION**. Every story and poem is keyed to an activity in a specific lesson, and where applicable, the selections are correlated for use in other chapters.

Copyright © 1994 Macmillan/McGraw-Hill School Publishing Company

All rights reserved. No part of this book may be reproduced or transmitted in any form or by any means, electronic or mechanical, including photocopying, recording, or by any information storage and retrieval system, without permission in writing from the publisher.

MACMILLAN/McGRAW-HILL SCHOOL DIVISION
10 UNION SQUARE EAST, NEW YORK, NEW YORK 10003

Printed in the United States of America

ISBN 0-02-109298-2 / 4

1 2 3 4 5 6 7 8 9 BAW 99 98 97 96 95 94 93

Illustration Credits: Diane Borowski 48, 49–55; Laura Cornell 3–4; Neverne Covington 8–9; David Diaz 5–6, 25–27, 40–47, 58; Allan Eitzen 7, 13–14, 33–37, 56; Richard Murdock 10–12, 38–39; Steven Nau 30–32; Hima Pamoedjo 57; Frank Riccio 16–19; Beata Szpura 15; Bea Weidner 20–24; Ron Zalme 2

Cover Illustration: Jenny Vainisi

ACKNOWLEDGMENTS

The publisher gratefully acknowledges permission to reprint the following copyrighted material:

"Setting a Limit," "Following a Formula" and "Jinxed or Not?" from ANY NUMBER CAN PLAY by George Sullivan. Text copyright © 1990 by George Sullivan. Reprinted by permission of HarperCollins Publishers.

"Decide for Yourself" from JATAKA TALES by Nancy DeRoin. Text copyright © 1975 by Nancy DeRoin. Reprinted by permission of Houghton Mifflin Co. All rights reserved.

ERNIE AND THE MILE-LONG MUFFLER by Marjorie Lewis. Text copyright © 1982 by Marjorie Lewis. Reprinted by permission of Marjorie Lewis.

"The Divided Students" and "The Farmer and the Merchant" from THE RICH MAN AND THE SINGER by Christine Price (ed.), told by Mesfin Habte-Mariam. Copyright © 1971 by Christine Price. Reprinted by permission of Dutton Children's Books, a division of Penguin Books USA Inc.

THE KING'S CHESSBOARD by David Birch. Text copyright © 1988 by David Birch. Reprinted by permission of Dial Books for Young Readers, a division of Penguin Books USA Inc.

Excerpt from "Lightening the Load" and "Telling the Horses Apart" from NOODLES, NITWITS, AND NUMSKULLS by Maria Leach. Copyright © 1961 by Maria Leach. Published by The World Publishing Company. Extensive research failed to locate the author and/or copyright holder for this work.

"Math Class" from THE MALIBU AND OTHER POEMS by Myra Cohn Livingston. Copyright © 1972 by Myra Cohn Livingston. Reprinted by permission of Marian Reiner for the author.

"The Race that was Rigged" from WHEN HIPPO WAS HAIRY by Nick Greaves. Copyright © 1988 by Nick Greaves. Reprinted by arrangement with Barron's Educational Series, Inc., Hauppauge, New York.

"Good Hotdogs" from MY WICKED, WICKED WAYS by Sandra Cisneros. Copyright © 1987 by Sandra Cisneros. Reprinted by permission of Third Woman Press.

WESLEY PAUL MARATHON RUNNER by Julianna A. Fogel. Text copyright © 1979 by Julianna A. Fogel. Reprinted by permission of HarperCollins Publishers.

"Pocket Calculator" by Bobbi Katz. Copyright © 1984 by Bobbi Katz. Used with permission of Bobbi Katz, who controls all rights.

"Don't Make a Bargain With a Fox" from THE KING OF THE MOUNTAINS: A Treasury of Latin American Folk Stories by M.A. Jagendorf and R.S. Boggs. Copyright © 1960 by M. A. Jagendorf and R. S. Boggs. Copyright renewed 1988 by Andre Jagendorf, Merna Alpert and R. S. Boggs. Reprinted by permission of Vanguard Press, a division of Random House, Inc.

(Acknowledgments continue on page 66)

•CONTENTS•

Setting a Limit
a nonfiction selection from *Any Number Can Play*
by George Sullivan **2**

Good Hotdogs
a poem by Sandra Cisneros **3**

Jinxed or Not?
a nonfiction selection from *Any Number Can Play*
by George Sullivan **5**

Following a Formula
a nonfiction selection from *Any Number Can Play*
by George Sullivan **7**

How the Terrapin Beat the Rabbit
a Native American folktale from *Cherokee Animal Tales*
edited by George F. Scheer **8**

The Race that was Rigged
a Swazi story from *When Hippo Was Hairy and Other Tales from Africa*
told by Nick Greaves **10**

The Farmer and the Merchant
a folktale from Ethiopia from *The Rich Man and the Singer: Folktales from Ethiopia*
told by Mesfin Habte-Mariam **13**

Pocket Calculator
a poem by Bobbi Katz **15**

The Wonderful Wooden Clock
a selection from the biography *Benjamin Banneker: Genius of Early America*
by Lillie Patterson **16**

Wesley Paul, Marathon Runner
a biography by Julianna A. Fogel **20**

Don't Make a Bargain With a Fox
a folktale from Argentina from *The King of the Mountains: A Treasury of Latin American Folktales* by M. A. Jagendorf and R. S. Boggs 25

Decide for Yourself
a Jataka tale from India retold by Nancy DeRoin 28

Ode to Los Raspados
a poem by Gary Soto 30

The King's Chessboard
a story from ancient India by David Birch 33

The Divided Students
a folktale from Ethiopia told by Mesfin Habte-Mariam 38

Grandfather Tang's Story
a story based on a Chinese folktale by Ann Tompert 40

Telling the Horses Apart
a North American folktale retold by Maria Leach 48

Ernie and the Mile-Long Muffler
a story by Marjorie Lewis 49

Lightening the Load
a North American folktale retold by Maria Leach 56

Math Class
a poem by Myra Cohn Livingston 57

Multiplication
a poem from *Arithmetic in Verse and Rhyme* selected by Allan and Leland Jacobs 58

Index 59

USING THE ANTHOLOGY

This chart correlates the Anthology selections to the 1994 Grade 4 *Mathematics in Action* program. Boldface type indicates where the selection is used in the Teacher's Edition of the program.

SELECTION	PAGE	CHAPTER(S)
Setting a Limit a nonfiction selection	2	Chapter **1**
Good Hotdogs a poem	3	Chapters **1**, 3, 5
Jinxed or Not? a nonfiction selection	5	Chapter **1**
Following a Formula a nonfiction selection	7	Chapter **1**
How the Terrapin Beat the Rabbit a Native American folktale	8	Chapter **2**
The Race that was Rigged a Swazi story	10	Chapters **2**, 9
The Farmer and the Merchant a folktale from Ethiopia	13	Chapters **3**, 12
Pocket Calculator a poem	15	Chapters 2, **3**, 5, 10
The Wonderful Wooden Clock a biography	16	Chapter **4**
Wesley Paul, Marathon Runner a biography	20	Chapters 2, 3, **4**, 9
Don't Make a Bargain With a Fox a folktale from Argentina	25	Chapters 5, **10**

SELECTION	PAGE	CHAPTER(S)
Decide for Yourself a Jataka tale from India	28	Chapters **5**, 10
Ode to Los Raspados a poem	30	Chapters 1, **6**
The King's Chessboard a story from ancient India	33	Chapters **6**, 10, 12
The Divided Students a folktale from Ethiopia	38	Chapters **7**, 9
Grandfather Tang's Story a story based on a Chinese folktale	40	Chapter **8**
Telling the Horses Apart a North American folktale	48	Chapter **9**
Ernie and the Mile-Long Muffler a story	49	Chapters 3, **9**, 12
Lightening the Load a North American folktale	56	Chapter **10**
Math Class a poem	57	Chapter **11**
Multiplication a poem	58	Chapters 5, **12**

STORIES & POEMS

Use with Chapter 1, Lesson 1

MATH CONNECTION
Number Sense

Setting a Limit

BY GEORGE SULLIVAN

In this selection, George Sullivan explains why a number higher than 5 never appears on a basketball uniform.

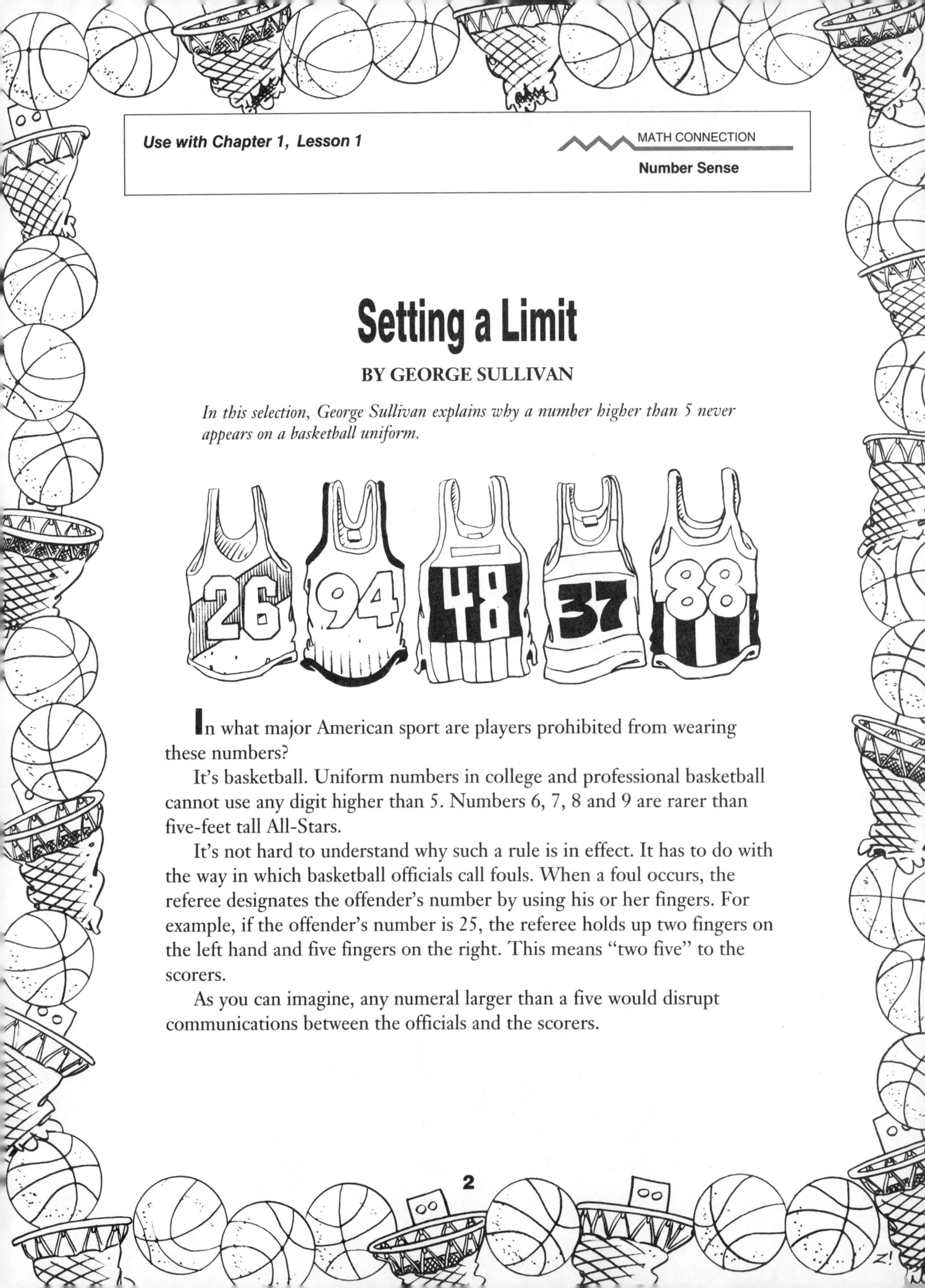

In what major American sport are players prohibited from wearing these numbers?

It's basketball. Uniform numbers in college and professional basketball cannot use any digit higher than 5. Numbers 6, 7, 8 and 9 are rarer than five-feet tall All-Stars.

It's not hard to understand why such a rule is in effect. It has to do with the way in which basketball officials call fouls. When a foul occurs, the referee designates the offender's number by using his or her fingers. For example, if the offender's number is 25, the referee holds up two fingers on the left hand and five fingers on the right. This means "two five" to the scorers.

As you can imagine, any numeral larger than a five would disrupt communications between the officials and the scorers.

Use with Chapter 1, Lesson 6

MATH CONNECTIONS

Money
Addition
Subtraction
Multiplication
Division

Good Hotdogs

BY SANDRA CISNEROS

"Good Hotdogs" gives students the opportunity to work with money and all operations — that is, if the description of the hot dogs doesn't make them rush out the door to buy their own!

Fifty cents apiece
To eat our lunch
We'd run
Straight from school
Instead of home
Two blocks
Then the store
That smelled like steam
You ordered
Because you had the money
Two hotdogs and two pops for here
Everything on the hotdogs
Except pickle lily
Dash those hotdogs
Into buns and splash on
All that good stuff

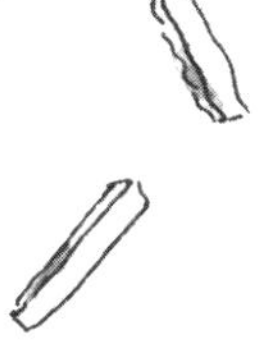

Yellow mustard and onions
And french fries piled on top all
Rolled up in a piece of wax
Paper for us to hold hot
In our hands
Quarters on the counter
Sit down
Good hotdogs
We'd eat
Fast till there was nothing left
But salt and poppy seeds even
The little burnt tips
Of french fries
We'd eat
You humming
And me swinging my legs

for Kiki

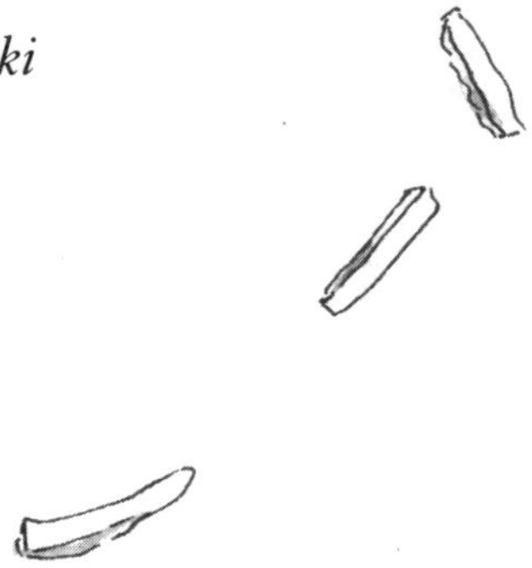

Use with Chapter 1, Lesson 9

MATH CONNECTION
Number Sense

Jinxed or Not?

BY GEORGE SULLIVAN

Add 1 ten and 3 ones and anything may happen! Poor number 13 is no more welcome on a professional sports uniform than it is on an elevator control panel. Students may enjoy researching triskaidekaphobia.

Fear of the number thirteen — what is known as triskaidekaphobia — is quite common. The floor-button panels in the elevators of many tall buildings often don't show a number thirteen. The panels read, ". . . 10, 11, 12, 14, 15 . . ."

Commercial airlines refuse to have a Flight 13. And aboard commercial airliners, there are no seats or rows of seats with that number.

In professional sports, jersey No. 13 is usually avoided. Most teams won't give out a jersey with that number unless a player insists upon wearing it.

Take professional football, for instance. Of the approximately 1,400 players listed on the rosters of the National Football League's twenty-eight teams in 1989, only six players felt courageous enough to wear No. 13.

The number is rarely seen in either professional basketball or hockey. Some seasons, No. 13 is not worn at all; other years, one or two players wear it.

Hockey players who shun No. 13 may have in mind what happened to Lars Lindgren, a defenseman with the Vancouver Canucks. Lindgren believed he was the victim of an injury jinx. To break the curse, Lindgren switched from a No. 3 jersey to a No. 13. His health improved, but during a game in November 1982 against the Edmonton Oilers, Lindgren shot the puck into his own net.

Despite such tales, there doesn't seem to be much solid evidence that wearing No. 13 is harmful to one's career. Baseball players frequently challenge the hex. In recent seasons, players who have worn the number have included: Ozzie Guillen, Chicago White Sox; Jeff Musselman, New York Mets; and Mike Pagliarulo, San Diego Padres.

Basketball's Wilt Chamberlain was another player who defied the No. 13 jinx. Chamberlain, who retired in 1972, still holds dozens of scoring records. These include the record for most points scored in a game (100) and most points scored in a season (4,029). In 1961-62, Chamberlain averaged 50.4 points per game, a record no other player has come close to. Chamberlain is one of the greatest players in basketball history, and some people hail him as *the* greatest. For Wilt Chamberlain No. 13 was anything but unlucky.

Use with Chapter 1, Lesson 12

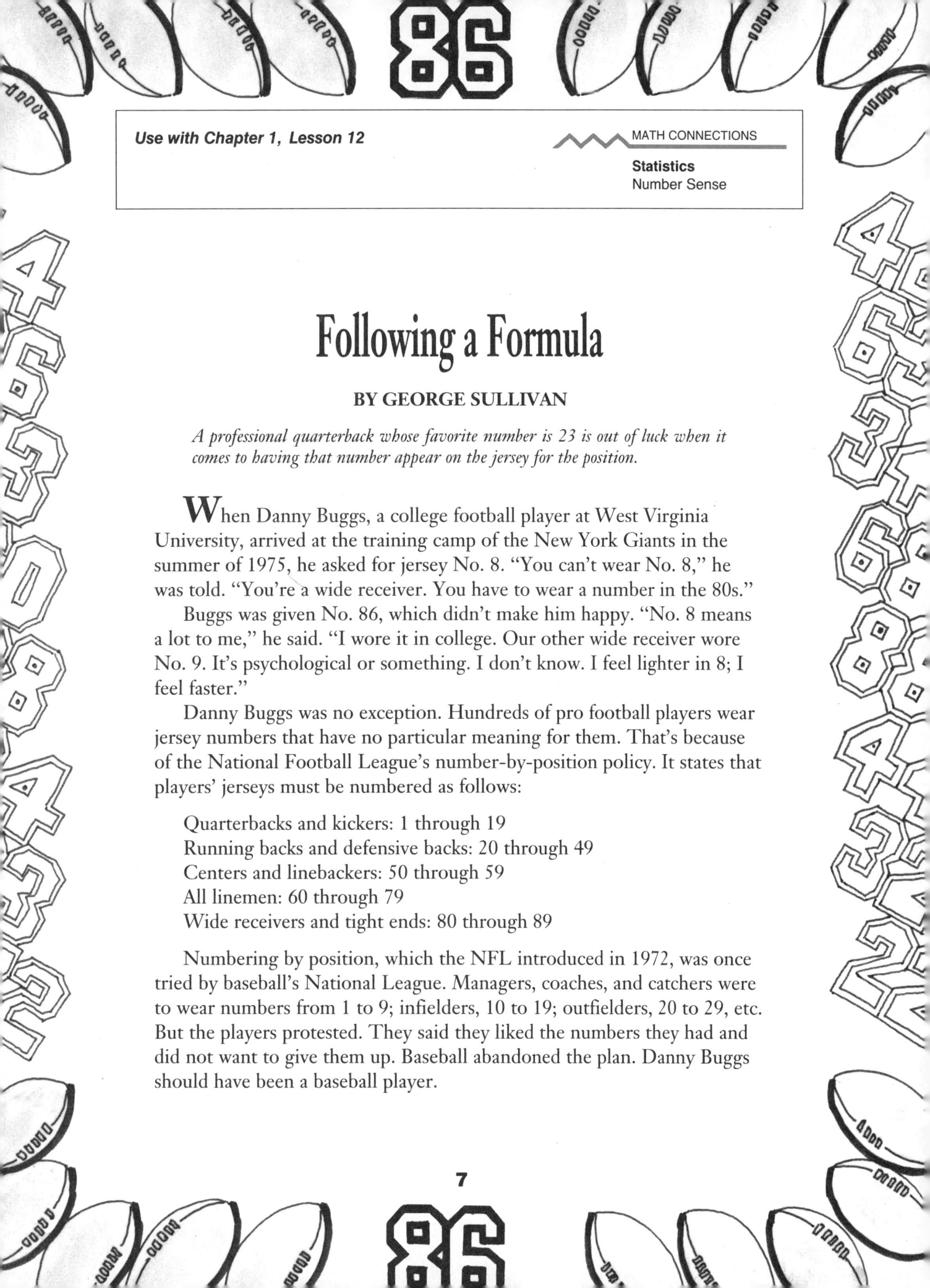

MATH CONNECTIONS
Statistics
Number Sense

Following a Formula

BY GEORGE SULLIVAN

A professional quarterback whose favorite number is 23 is out of luck when it comes to having that number appear on the jersey for the position.

When Danny Buggs, a college football player at West Virginia University, arrived at the training camp of the New York Giants in the summer of 1975, he asked for jersey No. 8. "You can't wear No. 8," he was told. "You're a wide receiver. You have to wear a number in the 80s."

Buggs was given No. 86, which didn't make him happy. "No. 8 means a lot to me," he said. "I wore it in college. Our other wide receiver wore No. 9. It's psychological or something. I don't know. I feel lighter in 8; I feel faster."

Danny Buggs was no exception. Hundreds of pro football players wear jersey numbers that have no particular meaning for them. That's because of the National Football League's number-by-position policy. It states that players' jerseys must be numbered as follows:

Quarterbacks and kickers: 1 through 19
Running backs and defensive backs: 20 through 49
Centers and linebackers: 50 through 59
All linemen: 60 through 79
Wide receivers and tight ends: 80 through 89

Numbering by position, which the NFL introduced in 1972, was once tried by baseball's National League. Managers, coaches, and catchers were to wear numbers from 1 to 9; infielders, 10 to 19; outfielders, 20 to 29, etc. But the players protested. They said they liked the numbers they had and did not want to give them up. Baseball abandoned the plan. Danny Buggs should have been a baseball player.

Use with Chapter 2, Lesson 1

MATH CONNECTIONS
Addition
Subtraction
Number Sense

CULTURAL CONNECTION
Cherokee Folktale

How the Terrapin Beat the Rabbit

FROM CHEROKEE ANIMAL TALES
EDITED BY GEORGE F. SCHEER

The story of the race between the tortoise and the hare appears in many cultures. The events and the outcome are always the same, but the characters of the two animals may be very different. In this Cherokee story, it is the terrapin that is boastful, rather than the rabbit.

The Rabbit was a great runner, and everybody knew it. No one thought the Terrapin was anything but a slow traveler. But he was a great warrior and very boastful, and he and the Rabbit were always disputing about their speed. At last, they agreed to decide who was the faster by running a race. They chose the day and a starting place and agreed to run across four mountain ridges to a finish line.

The Rabbit felt so sure of winning that he said to the Terrapin, "You know you can't run. You can never win the race. So I will give you a head start. You may start at the top of the first ridge. Then you'll have only three to cross, while I go over four."

The Terrapin said that that would be all right. But that night, when he went home to his family, he sent for his terrapin friends and told them he wanted their help. He said he knew he could not outrun the Rabbit, but he wanted to stop the Rabbit's boasting. He explained his plan to his friends. And they agreed to help him.

When the day of the race came, all the animals went out to watch. The Rabbit was with them. But the Terrapin had gone ahead toward the top of the first ridge, as he and the Rabbit had agreed. The animals could hardly see him, away in the tall grass.

The starting signal was given. The Rabbit ran with long jumps up the mountain, expecting to win the race before the Terrapin could get down the far side of that first ridge. But before the Rabbit got to the top of the mountain, he saw the Terrapin go over the ridge ahead of him. He ran on. When he reached the top, he looked around, but he could not see the Terrapin.

The Rabbit ran down the far side of the mountain and began to climb the second ridge. But when he looked up, there was the Terrapin just going over the top! The Rabbit was greatly surprised and made his longest jumps to catch up. But when he got to the top of that second ridge, there was the Terrapin, again far out in front, going over the third ridge! The Rabbit was getting tired now. He was nearly out of breath. But he kept on down the mountain and up the third ridge. He got to the top, just in time to see the Terrapin cross the fourth ridge and win the race!

The Rabbit could not make another jump. He fell over on the ground, crying, "Mi! mi! mi! mi!" as the Rabbit has done ever since when he is too tired to run any more.

The Terrapin was named the winner of the race — although all the animals wondered how he had won against the Rabbit.

The Terrapin kept quiet and never told. But it had been easy enough to win. All the Terrapin's friends looked just alike. He had placed one of them near the top of each ridge to wait until the Rabbit came in sight and then to climb over the ridge and hide in the long grass on the far side. As the Rabbit reached the top of each ridge, he would see a Terrapin going over the next ridge ahead. And though he could hardly believe his eyes, he thought his rival was always one ridge ahead of him. But, of course, it was not his rival he saw each time. It was one of his rival's friends.

Where was the Terrapin? Why, all the while, he was near the top of the fourth ridge, where he had gone before the race began. When the Rabbit ran over the third ridge, the Terrapin had simply popped over the fourth ridge and waddled down to the finish line, so that he would appear to be the one who won the race — and could answer questions if the animals suspected anything!

Use with Chapter 2, Lesson 9

MATH CONNECTION
Measurement

CULTURAL CONNECTION
Folktale from Africa

The Race that was Rigged

TOLD BY NICK GREAVES

This Swazi story from Africa about the tortoise and the hare is a read-aloud selection. You may wish to give synonyms for the words "ponderous," "earnest," and "plodded."

Tortoise was eating peacefully one day, minding his own business, when along came Mofuli, the hare. Mofuli, like all wicked little hares, could not resist the chance to make fun of Tortoise and tease him about how slow and ponderous he was.

Mofuli, full of mischief, challenged Tortoise to a race. There were some palm trees about 550 yards (500 metres) from where they were, and Mofuli said that was where they would race to.

Tortoise had had enough of Mofuli, and all hares, to last him a lifetime, since this was not the first time he had been teased by one of these irritating creatures. He wished he could put Hare in his place once and for all.

He thought for a moment and then said, "Speed is not everything, Mofuli. One must have endurance, too. Let us make this a real race — a long one. Let us race to the Blue Pan, some six miles (ten kilometres) from here. And, so that I have time to prepare, let us run the race in five days' time, at noon."

Mofuli was most surprised. He hadn't expected Tortoise to accept the challenge, and had been looking forward to a good long teasing. But he was scornful, and he almost decided not to bother with the race. But

Tortoise was so much in earnest, that in the end he agreed. And Hare went on his way, laughing. He could hardly wait to tell all the other animals about the silly old Tortoise.

But Tortoise lost no time. He called on his relatives for help, telling them about his plan. It was very simple: at noon on Saturday, they were to place themselves in different positions all along the path that Hare and Tortoise were to race. Every one of them was to run toward Blue Pan, starting from different points along the route. All they had to do was to keep going as fast as they could, until Hare had sped past, and then they could go home and rest if they wanted to.

Tortoise collected a gourd to hold water, and set off for the pan that very day. It took him almost five days to get to Blue Pan, but at last he arrived. At noon Saturday, he filled his gourd with water and settled down to wait.

Meanwhile Mofuli had arrived at the starting point at the agreed time, and there he found Tortoise's cousin. It did not occur to Mofuli that this was a different tortoise. They greeted each other, and the race began.

Mofuli was out of sight in a twinkling, and Tortoise's cousin plodded off on his way, chuckling to himself. Mofuli was laughing too, until he reached the first rise and there was Tortoise ahead of him! (Actually, it was Tortoise's brother, stumbling along as fast as he could go.) Mofuli ran faster and soon he was out of sight. He was rather puzzled, and as the race went on, he became more and more confused.

Over each hill, Mofuli found Tortoise in front of him. Each time he overtook him, running like the wind, Tortoise would laugh loudly. By now, Hare was thinking that Tortoise must have learned to fly.

It was very hot, being midday, and the sun beat down. The pan was still two miles (three kilometres) away, and Mofuli was terribly thirsty. He came over the next rise to find Tortoise, ahead of him again!

In desperation, Mofuli put on his last burst of speed. Heart pounding, he strained every muscle, and at last came in sight of the Blue Pan. He was almost at the pan, when suddenly he tripped and fell. He lay on the ground, exhausted — he could go no further. His sides were heaving and every limb was trembling.

After a few moments he staggered to his feet. He looked up and what do you think he saw?

Why, Tortoise, of course, walking towards him from the pan, carrying a gourd of cool, clear water. This sight was more than Mofuli could stand. He fainted from shock and exhaustion.

Tortoise revived Hare by sprinkling cold water over his face. When Mofuli came round, Tortoise said in a soothing voice, "Drink this, my poor friend. I had an idea that you might be needing it. The endurance of some animals is not quite what they claim it to be." And he chuckled quietly to himself.

So it was that slow old Tortoise beat Hare at his own game. Clever as he was, Mofuli did not have the brains to see that he himself had at last been made a fool of.

Use with Chapter 3, Lesson 1

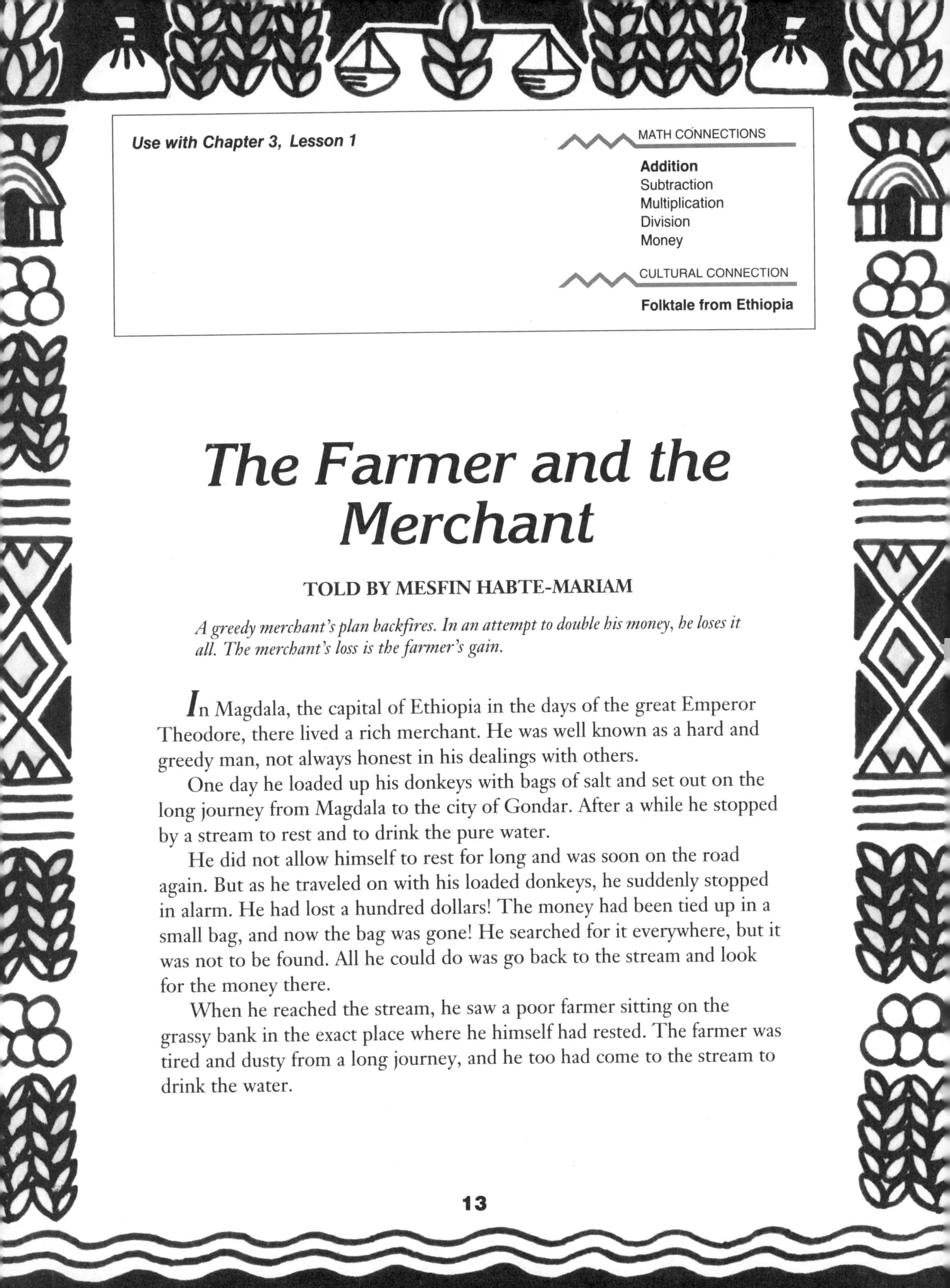

MATH CONNECTIONS

Addition
Subtraction
Multiplication
Division
Money

CULTURAL CONNECTION

Folktale from Ethiopia

The Farmer and the Merchant

TOLD BY MESFIN HABTE-MARIAM

A greedy merchant's plan backfires. In an attempt to double his money, he loses it all. The merchant's loss is the farmer's gain.

In Magdala, the capital of Ethiopia in the days of the great Emperor Theodore, there lived a rich merchant. He was well known as a hard and greedy man, not always honest in his dealings with others.

One day he loaded up his donkeys with bags of salt and set out on the long journey from Magdala to the city of Gondar. After a while he stopped by a stream to rest and to drink the pure water.

He did not allow himself to rest for long and was soon on the road again. But as he traveled on with his loaded donkeys, he suddenly stopped in alarm. He had lost a hundred dollars! The money had been tied up in a small bag, and now the bag was gone! He searched for it everywhere, but it was not to be found. All he could do was go back to the stream and look for the money there.

When he reached the stream, he saw a poor farmer sitting on the grassy bank in the exact place where he himself had rested. The farmer was tired and dusty from a long journey, and he too had come to the stream to drink the water.

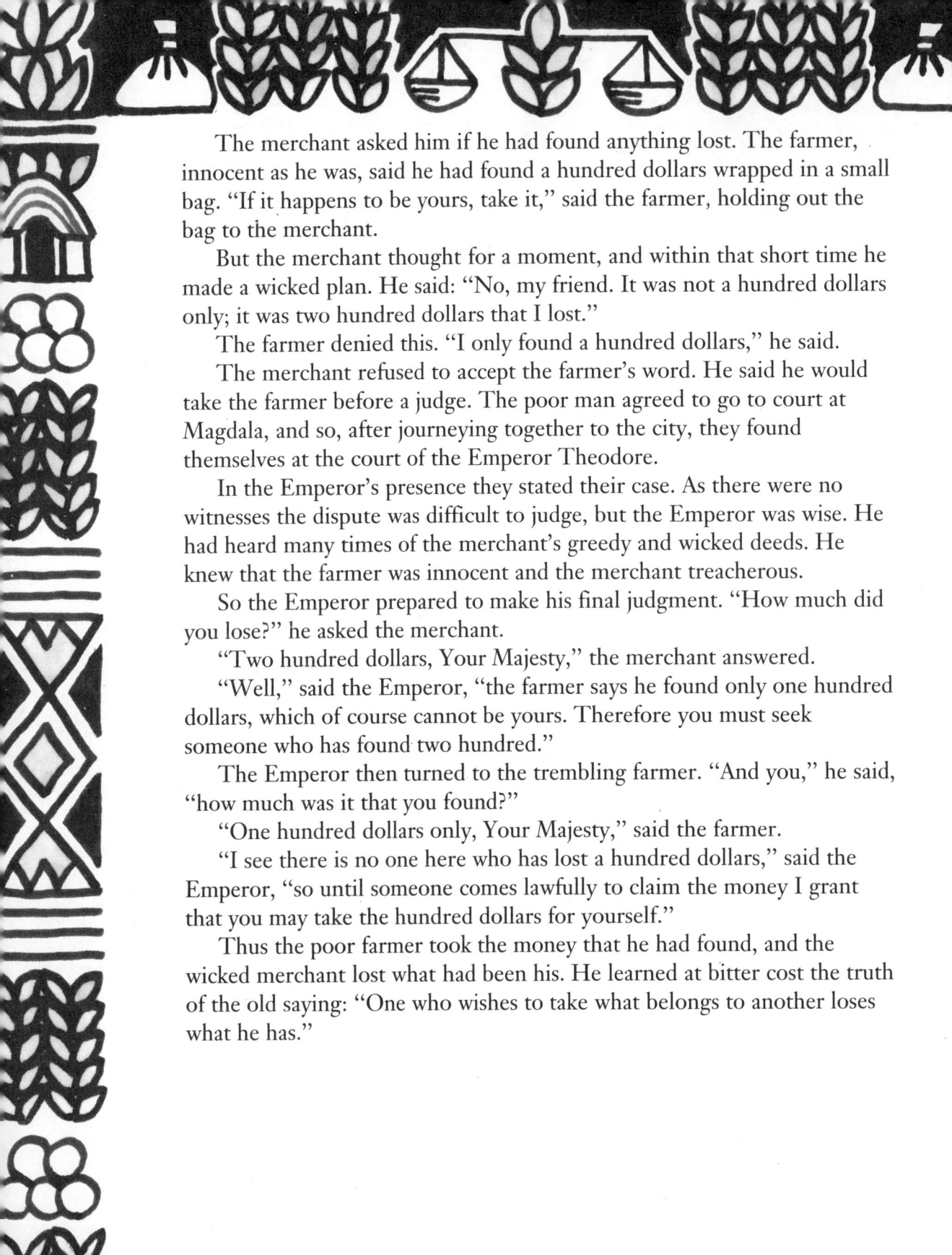

The merchant asked him if he had found anything lost. The farmer, innocent as he was, said he had found a hundred dollars wrapped in a small bag. "If it happens to be yours, take it," said the farmer, holding out the bag to the merchant.

But the merchant thought for a moment, and within that short time he made a wicked plan. He said: "No, my friend. It was not a hundred dollars only; it was two hundred dollars that I lost."

The farmer denied this. "I only found a hundred dollars," he said.

The merchant refused to accept the farmer's word. He said he would take the farmer before a judge. The poor man agreed to go to court at Magdala, and so, after journeying together to the city, they found themselves at the court of the Emperor Theodore.

In the Emperor's presence they stated their case. As there were no witnesses the dispute was difficult to judge, but the Emperor was wise. He had heard many times of the merchant's greedy and wicked deeds. He knew that the farmer was innocent and the merchant treacherous.

So the Emperor prepared to make his final judgment. "How much did you lose?" he asked the merchant.

"Two hundred dollars, Your Majesty," the merchant answered.

"Well," said the Emperor, "the farmer says he found only one hundred dollars, which of course cannot be yours. Therefore you must seek someone who has found two hundred."

The Emperor then turned to the trembling farmer. "And you," he said, "how much was it that you found?"

"One hundred dollars only, Your Majesty," said the farmer.

"I see there is no one here who has lost a hundred dollars," said the Emperor, "so until someone comes lawfully to claim the money I grant that you may take the hundred dollars for yourself."

Thus the poor farmer took the money that he had found, and the wicked merchant lost what had been his. He learned at bitter cost the truth of the old saying: "One who wishes to take what belongs to another loses what he has."

Use with Chapter 3, Lesson 12

MATH CONNECTIONS
Addition
Subtraction
Number Sense

Pocket Calculator

BY BOBBI KATZ

The best method of calculation to use at the beach (when you're waist-high in the waves) may not be a calculator. This poem may help stimulate students' thinking about the circumstances in which a calculator is the best choice.

Add them up!
   Subtract!
      Divide!
Your magic brain is tucked inside
A teeny, weeny, boxy space
With numbers written on your face.
My brain is so much bigger, yet
It fumbles answers you can get,
And you must think it's very slow
At finding out stuff that you know.
(But when it's time to read a poem
Or dash into the ocean's foam
I calculate I'll leave you home!)

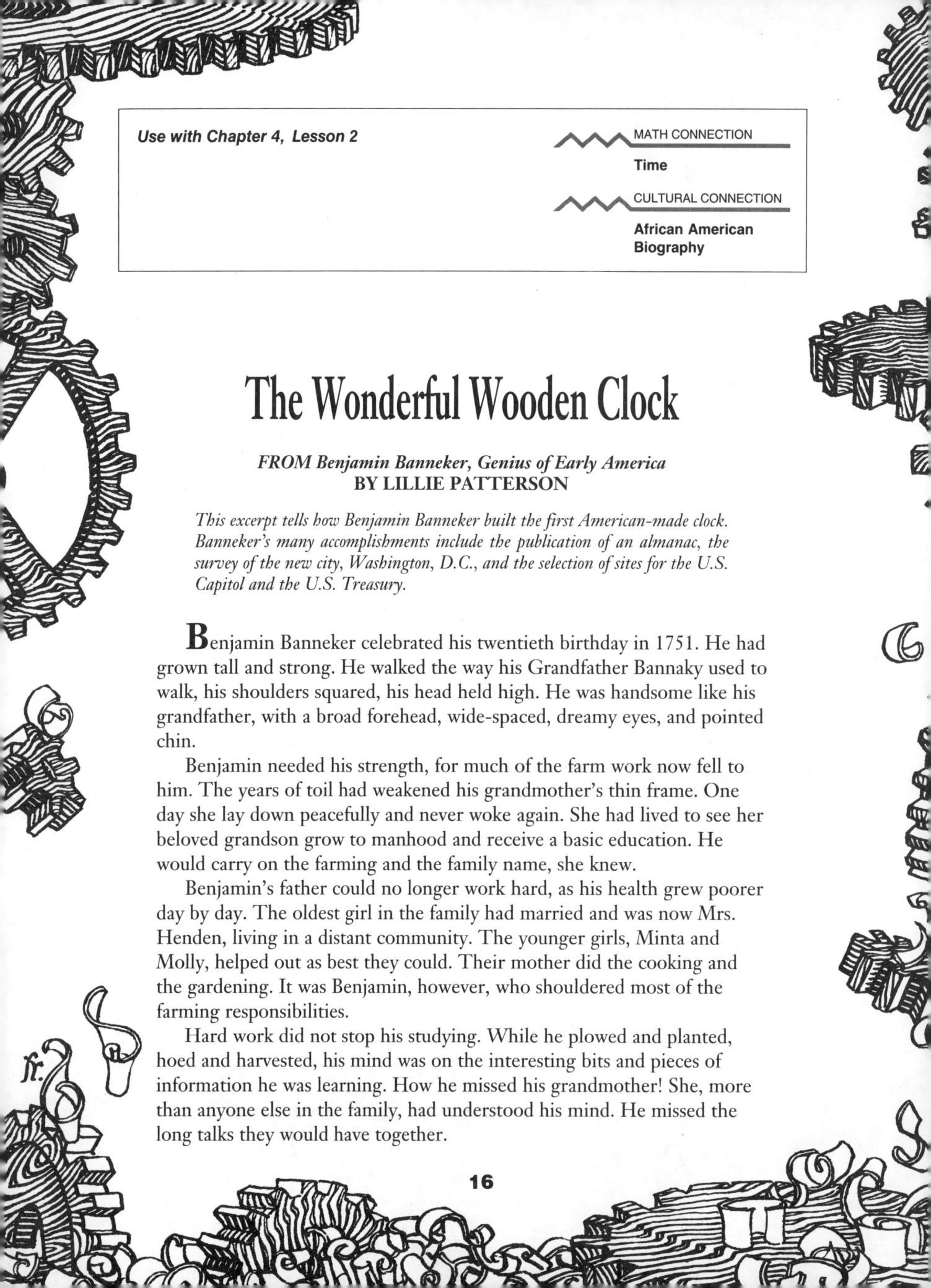

Use with Chapter 4, Lesson 2

MATH CONNECTION
Time

CULTURAL CONNECTION
African American Biography

The Wonderful Wooden Clock

FROM Benjamin Banneker, Genius of Early America
BY LILLIE PATTERSON

This excerpt tells how Benjamin Banneker built the first American-made clock. Banneker's many accomplishments include the publication of an almanac, the survey of the new city, Washington, D.C., and the selection of sites for the U.S. Capitol and the U.S. Treasury.

Benjamin Banneker celebrated his twentieth birthday in 1751. He had grown tall and strong. He walked the way his Grandfather Bannaky used to walk, his shoulders squared, his head held high. He was handsome like his grandfather, with a broad forehead, wide-spaced, dreamy eyes, and pointed chin.

Benjamin needed his strength, for much of the farm work now fell to him. The years of toil had weakened his grandmother's thin frame. One day she lay down peacefully and never woke again. She had lived to see her beloved grandson grow to manhood and receive a basic education. He would carry on the farming and the family name, she knew.

Benjamin's father could no longer work hard, as his health grew poorer day by day. The oldest girl in the family had married and was now Mrs. Henden, living in a distant community. The younger girls, Minta and Molly, helped out as best they could. Their mother did the cooking and the gardening. It was Benjamin, however, who shouldered most of the farming responsibilities.

Hard work did not stop his studying. While he plowed and planted, hoed and harvested, his mind was on the interesting bits and pieces of information he was learning. How he missed his grandmother! She, more than anyone else in the family, had understood his mind. He missed the long talks they would have together.

To fill the void left by his grandmother's death, Benjamin concentrated upon the study of mathematics. He especially liked algebra and geometry, for they challenged his thinking. As he got to know the neighboring farmers, he used his skill with numbers to help them. Many of these farmers had never been to school and could not read or write. Benjamin showed them how to weigh their tobacco properly, and he assisted them in figuring the value of their tobacco receipts.

He would meet these farmers when he went to the river landings to sell or trade tobacco from his own farm. One morning he got up unusually early and dressed in his best clothes. Because of his friendship and admiration for his Quaker teacher, he adopted many of the Quaker customs and ways of thinking. He usually wore a long, plain coat and a broadbrimmed hat, the familiar dress of Quaker men.

"I am off to Elk Ridge Landing," Benjamin told his mother. "Many tobacco merchants will be coming there today." He mounted his favorite horse and rode away.

At the landing, he met a merchant with whom he liked to trade. As the two talked, the merchant suddenly took something from his pocket.

Benjamin stared at the object, his eyes wide with interest. "May I see that?" he asked, forgetting all about the business at hand.

"Of course you may see my pocket watch." The merchant held the timepiece on his palm. "I ordered it from England last year," he said. "Have you never seen a watch before?"

"Never!" Benjamin bent his head to look closer. "I have seen a sundial, but never a clock or a watch. May I hold it for a moment?"

The watch in Benjamin's hand seemed almost alive, ticking as though it breathed. He watched the tiny hands move slowly around and around, marking off the minutes. Holding the pocket watch to his ear, he listened to the regular rhythm of its movements.

A new adventure in learning was about to begin. The thought of the watch made Benjamin dizzy with excitement. He knew that many rich people in the colonies owned clocks and watches, but they lived in cities. He knew of no clock in the rural area where he lived. Yet he was holding a real timepiece in his hand.

The kind merchant was struck by the black man's interest in his watch. "Would you like to borrow it for a few weeks?" he asked. "You could return it when you come to sell me your tobacco."

"Yes, yes, thank you," Benjamin answered. "I will treasure it like a jewel."

He rode home, his mind whirling with new ideas. As he moved along, he measured his horse's gait to the tick-ticking in his pocket.

Minta and Molly met him, astonished to see the treasure their brother had brought. That night the family watched while Benjamin put the watch on the table and began to study it. A few nights later, they stared in disbelief as he picked up a small knife. Working ever so carefully, he began to pry the back from the watch.

The two sisters leaned over Benjamin's shoulders, scarcely breathing. "You're not going to take it apart?" Molly asked.

"How else will I discover how it works?" he retorted, never taking his eyes from the watch.

"Can you put the pieces back together?" Minta worried.

Benjamin grinned. "Anything I can take apart, I can put together again."

Every night that week he sat studying the inner workings of the timepiece. He marveled at the tiny gears and wheels, observing the way they moved. Working like an artist, he drew each part—the wheels, the gears, the springs. By the time he returned the watch to the merchant several weeks later, his drawings were finished. He had memorized every detail of the watch, inside and outside.

"What now?" Benjamin's father asked him.

"It's time for me to do some figuring," Benjamin decided. "I know enough mathematics to figure out plans for the clock I will make."

"A clock?" The family looked at Benjamin as though he had lost his mind.

"What will you use?" his mother wanted to know.

Benjamin never blinked an eye. "I will use what I have."

What he had, and plenty of it, was wood. He picked out pieces of hard-grained wood and seasoned them well. After the harvest was over that year, he began to whittle away at the wood.

During the winter days, when fields lay resting under frost or snow and the fire roared in the chimney, Benjamin cut and whittled the pieces of wood. His knowledge of mathematics served him well. Careful mathematical calculations had to be made in order to determine the size of each part of the clock he planned.

Every part had to be precisely cut and measured. First Benjamin carved the teeth of the wheelwork. This alone took months. Time after time he made the wheels, only to find that the parts did not fit together properly. Patiently, he would put the old parts aside and start to make new ones.

Spring returned, and it was planting time. Benjamin worked in the fields by day and labored over his clock at night. Sometimes the parts proved too big, sometimes they were too small. "This is much like a puzzle," Benjamin told his family. "I never give up on any puzzle until I have solved it."

Finally the day came when all the parts were finished. With a sigh of relief, Benjamin began to put them together.

"Oh, no!" His groan of disappointment told the story. The hour and the minute hands moved, but they did not move in a way to tell perfect time. No matter how well Benjamin had made each separate part, he knew that all parts had to work as a unit. Only then could his clock tell time correctly.

The amateur clockmaker refused to give up. Over and over he used his calculations — figuring, measuring, cutting, thinking. For well-nigh two years he labored over the clock. At last, late one night, his family heard him give a cry of triumph.

"They fit!" All the parts worked together — as perfectly as the pieces of a neat puzzle. The clock was made entirely of wood except for the striking parts, which had to be made from iron and brass.

At first Benjamin set the clock to strike every hour. Finding that this loud striking kept the family awake at night, he adjusted the workings to strike at six and again at twelve.

Happily, Benjamin made a sturdy case and a dial for his timepiece. Then he hung it on the wall beside the fireplace.

So it was that in 1753, at age twenty-two, Benjamin Banneker made the first striking clock with all parts made entirely in America. Other clocks had been made in the colonies, no doubt, but at least some of the parts had been made in Europe. Most of the colonial clockmakers had been trained in England.

Word of the wonderful wooden clock spread rapidly. People came from miles around to see the marvel.

"Amazing!" some visitors said, gazing at the timepiece. "What expert craftsmanship."

"Unbelievable!" others cried, looking at the young black man who had made it. "Benjamin Banneker is a genius."

The fame of the clockmaker spread all over the Patapsco Valley and beyond. The clock became one of the wonders of the day. Benjamin, the farmer, became better known as Banneker, the inventor.

Use with Chapter 4, Lesson 3

MATH CONNECTIONS

Time
Measurement
Addition
Subtraction

Wesley Paul, Marathon Runner

BY JULIANNA A. FOGEL

Wesley Paul is a nine-year-old marathoner. This story recounts his training for the marathons in Chicago and New York City. Activities on subtracting larger numbers and adding and subtracting units of measure as well as time may be initiated by Wesley's training schedule and marathon performances.

My name is Wesley Paul. I'm nine years old. When I was three, my dad started jogging to lose weight, and he took me along. I've been running ever since.

At first, I ran just for fun. I didn't keep track of how far or how fast I could go. But then I began to enjoy doing a little better each time, and I got serious about it.

A lot of kids can run fast for short distances, but running long distances is really different from sprints across the playground. You have to train, build your endurance and strength. I run at least ten miles every day.

The kids in my class ask me to race at recess, but I try to get out of it, because I'm kind of shy and I don't want to make a big deal of my running. It's better if I stick to four-square, where we can all have fun.

When I get home from school, I have a glass of milk and talk to my mother and my brother Darcy. Darcy is two. Sometimes he comes out and tries to run with me, but he can't keep up because he's still too little. If he was closer to my age, we could do more things together.

After my snack, I change my clothes and get ready to work out.

First, I warm up with twenty or thirty different stretch exercises — some to the side, some forward; some standing, some sitting. There seems to be an exercise for every single muscle. Doing them isn't much fun, but it's important. One time when I didn't warm up before running, I pulled a muscle. I couldn't run for four days.

I work out every day, winter and summer. The only time I get bored is when the weather is really bad and I have to run indoors. It's easy to lose count of my distance when I'm going around and around on the same flat track.

My dad is my coach. He decides which races I should enter, and he plans all my training. He maps different routes for me and clocks my workouts with a stopwatch.

Mostly I train on a golf course, which is pretty flat. Some days Dad has me run hills. Hills can be killers for a runner, but I try to think of them as friends. They are great for building up your legs and wind. Many runners can't keep their pace going uphill, so hills can be great places to pass other runners in races.

The longest race I run is the marathon. A long time ago, in Greece, a soldier ran to Athens from another city called Marathon to bring news of his army's victory. The marathon is the same distance that soldier ran — 26 miles, 385 yards. So far, I have run in seven marathons.

One week before I run a marathon, I run 20 miles without stopping. If I can run that far, I know I'll be able to run 26 miles, 385 yards — or even farther. I got lost once during a marathon, and when I finally found the finish line I learned I had covered 33 miles. Boy, was I mad!

Once, the summer I was eight, I had to drop out of a marathon — but that was because I was hit by a car. At the 6-mile mark, the car's outside mirror slammed into me.

I had trained for that race all summer, hoping to break the national record for eight-year-olds. I wanted to keep going, but I couldn't. The stitches I got in the back of my head didn't hurt nearly as much as the disappointment inside.

My dad knew how I felt. He said, "Wesley, if you recover in time, we'll enter the Mayor Daley Marathon in Chicago."

I wasn't so sure how I would do in Chicago. I had never run in a marathon in a big city. The race was only two weeks away, and I couldn't train for it because of the accident.

I did okay. I finished 250th out of 5,000 runners, and I won a trophy for my age division. But I didn't break the record for eight-year-olds.

After the Chicago race, I felt kind of let down. I kept thinking, "I could have broken that record, if only I hadn't been hit by that dumb car."

About two weeks later, I got an invitation to run in the New York City Marathon. I was very excited about it. Runners don't usually get special invitations to be in a race; they just sign up. I was invited because I had done well in Chicago. The New York race is really big and important. Best of all, it was another chance for me to break the national record.

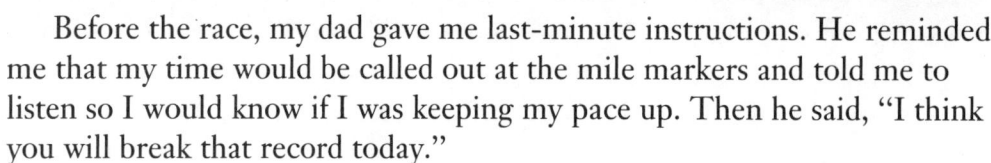

Before the race, my dad gave me last-minute instructions. He reminded me that my time would be called out at the mile markers and told me to listen so I would know if I was keeping my pace up. Then he said, "I think you will break that record today."

And I did! I ran the marathon in 3 hours, 31 seconds. I broke the record by 15 whole minutes.

Before long, I began thinking about running a marathon even faster. During the whole next year I worked to build up my speed and strength. I ran in a lot of shorter races and trained hard.

All my training was aimed at a new goal: to finish a marathon in under three hours.

I had been looking forward to the New York City Marathon for weeks. I guess that's why I was so nervous. The race wasn't supposed to begin until 10:30 in the morning, but I made sure we were there by 7:00.

I was worried about the weather. Perfect weather for running a marathon is between 40 and 50 degrees Fahrenheit, and cloudy. But the forecast was for 75 degrees and sunny. It's awful to run when it's hot, because your body loses so much liquid when you perspire.

I checked my socks and shoes very carefully. I made sure that my heels were all the way back in the shoes and that there were no wrinkles in the socks, so I wouldn't get blisters. I tied the laces in double knots. Something was doing the same to my stomach.

Then I did stretch exercises for about an hour. I kept remembering the dream I had had the night before. It was terrible. I was running in the New York City Marathon. It was boiling hot, and I quit at the 5-mile mark. My time was three hours, but I had gone only five miles. All the runners were dropping out, as if we were all under a spell . . . .

I wished there was a machine with a switch I could turn to control the weather.

Lots of runners meditate before a race. Some people try to make their minds go blank. But I think about the race, every single step I think about my pace and about how I'm going to breathe, and I imagine how I will feel at the 5-mile mark . . . the 15 . . . the 20. I run the whole race in my mind, if I can.

An older kid came up and asked me, "What's your time going to be?"

I said, "Less than three hours."

He said, "You're kidding."

I told him I wasn't.

Then he asked me for advice, because he'd never run in a marathon before.

Big city . . . big race . . . big butterflies! The worst part of a marathon is standing around waiting. It seemed like forever before the starting cannon went off.

Boom! I heard something else that sounded like a huge roar, but it was just the crowd cheering.

We started up slowly. There were so many runners I could hardly move.

After about two miles, the runners finally began to spread out. I didn't feel so crowded, and running was easier.

Some runners hold back at the start of a marathon because they are afraid they'll get tired too quickly. I've never done that. I try to keep my pace steady.

In order to break three hours, I had to run each mile of the marathon in 6 minutes, 30 seconds.

The next ten miles clicked off fast. It was pretty quiet. Some of the runners were talking back and forth, but I didn't talk to anyone. I just listened to the sound of other runners breathing and shoes thumping on the pavement, and concentrated on my pace.

I had lots of time to think. I thought about music and made up tunes and hummed them. I worked math problems in my head. I took the number of miles I had run and multiplied it by six and one-half, to keep track of how much time should have passed.

By the 15-mile mark, I was hot and thirsty. My legs had begun to feel sore, as if some invisible hammer was hitting them. I thought, "I still have over eleven miles to go."

Then some boy yelled, "Hey, kid! What are you doing in this race? You'll never make it. Why don't you just quit now?"

He did me a real favor. He made me more determined than ever to break three hours.

Lots of runners talk about "hitting the wall" during a marathon. It means reaching a point where all your energy is gone and you feel as if you're trying to run through a brick wall. It usually happens sometimes during the last six miles.

I hit the wall at the 22-mile mark. All of a sudden, I felt as if I couldn't take another step. That's what it must be like to be zapped by a laser gun. I felt paralyzed.

All around me, runners were dropping out, just like in my dream. I thought, "I can't move." But somehow I kept going.

At the 25-mile mark, I heard the crowd yelling. This time it was encouragement: "C'mon! You can do it! Go!"

I told myself, "Wesley, you're almost finished. Run!"

Soon I could see the big clock at the finish line. When I got close enough to read what it said, I couldn't believe it.

Two hours, 59 minutes!

As I crossed the finish line, somebody rushed up to me, handed me a medal, and said, "Good job!"

All the months of training had paid off. In spite of the heat, I had broken three hours.

All the runners who finished were wrapped in foil so we wouldn't cool off too quickly. I was so tired it seemed unreal. And I had gotten a big blister after all.

But it felt wonderful to have reached my goal.

Of course, there's always another race to win, another record to break — even if it's your own.

What I really want to do is try out for the Olympics when I'm old enough.

But there is more to running than winning races and breaking records. Running is fun. It makes you feel good. You can run with a friend, or go alone if you feel like being by yourself. You can set your own pace. And you don't need a lot of equipment.

All you have to do is walk out the door and start.

Use with Chapter 10, Lesson 1

MATH CONNECTION
Fractions
Division

CULTURAL CONNECTION
Folktale from Argentina

Don't Make a Bargain With a Fox

FROM The King of the Mountains
BY M. A. JAGENDORF AND R. S. BOGGS

Two small animals are left out in the cold when they make a bargain with a fox. If students do not understand the Spanish word compadres *within the context of the story, explain that in English it means friends or companions.*

Sometime back, long ago, two *viscachas*—rodent animals, about the size of a hare—lived together in the brush of the Argentina pampas. They were good friends, and they were always together. One day they were scampering along over the stubble and the grass, smelling this and smelling that, and now and then stopping to do a little gnawing. It was pleasant for them to live on the great pampas of Argentina.

Suddenly they saw two red blotches. They ran up to them carefully—you never can tell what you'll meet on the pampas. They went up to those red blotches and sniffed. They were two pieces of a ragged red blanket someone had left, either forgotten or thrown away.

"This is a valuable treasure," said one.

"Some Indian must have forgotten it and left it here. Or maybe he didn't know he dropped it," said the other.

"In any case, we've found it and it's ours," said the first.

"Yes, it's ours. What shall we do with it?"

"Well, I know. Let's use it for a blanket. We can cover ourselves with it when it's cold."

"That's a good idea. But, look, I'm lying on one piece all stretched out, and it's too small."

25

"Yes, it is too small, but we can sew the two pieces together."

"Yes, we could do that, but where can we find a needle and some thread?"

"That's a thought. I haven't any, and you haven't either."

"What shall we do?"

"I don't know."

They sat looking at each other, wiggling their sharp little noses up and down.

Just then Señor Fox came along. He had a long nose and a long tail, and a keen brain in his head besides.

"*Buenos días*, good day, my good friends," he said. "You look worried. Is anything wrong?"

"Yes!" they both said at once. "We need a needle and some thread to sew together these two pieces of our fine new blanket."

"What will you do with it after you have sewed it?"

"We'll cover ourselves with it on cold nights," they both answered. "It will keep us warm."

"I'll give you a needle and some thread if you'll let me share your fine blanket."

"That we will, just give us the needle and thread."

Señor Fox gave them the needle and thread, and they went to work. In a short time the two pieces were sewed together.

"You have done a fine piece of work," said Señor Fox. "Now give me back my needle. I'll see you tonight." Then he went away.

The little viscachas ran around and picked up bits of food here and there. Night came, and the cold wind began to blow all over the pampas.

"This is the time of year when our blanket will feel good," they said, and they were very pleased with themselves.

Señor Fox came loping along. "Good evening, my good little friends," he said.

"Good evening, *buenas noches*, Señor Fox."

"It's a cold night, *compadres*."

"Yes, it is a cold night, Señor Fox."

"But *we* won't be cold, *compadres*. You have that fine blanket for which I lent you my needle and thread. If it weren't for me, you wouldn't have a blanket at all, so I have as much right to it as you do."

"Yes, that's true, Señor Fox."

"Now, let's see," Señor Fox said, and scratched his head. "Let's see. I gave you the needle and I gave you the thread, and you used my thread to sew it down the middle, so the middle is really my part."

"That sounds right, Señor Fox."

"Then the right thing is for me to lie under the middle part, which is my part, and for you two to be on the sides, which are your parts."

"That sounds right, Señor Fox."

So Señor Fox lay down on the ground, and the two viscachas put the middle of the blanket over him. Then they lay down, one on each side of him.

Now, you know that Señor Fox is large and wide, so the blanket covered him, but there was little left to cover the two poor viscachas lying on either side. Each one had only one edge of the blanket, which barely reached halfway across his body, leaving the other half out in the cold wind. And that's the way they had to lie, shivering all night long.

So you see that you can never strike a bargain with a fox. He'll get the best of you every time.

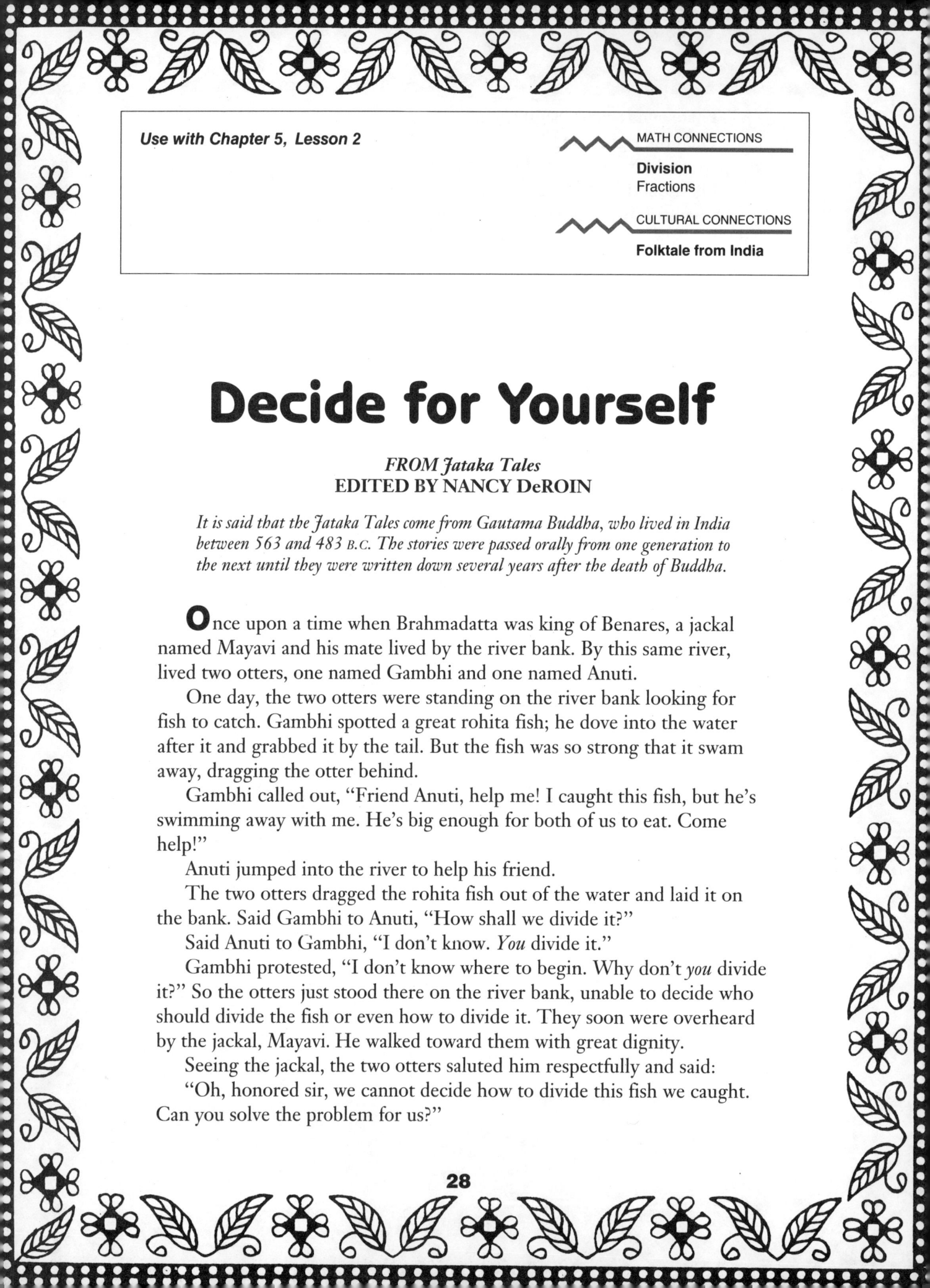

Use with Chapter 5, Lesson 2

MATH CONNECTIONS
Division
Fractions

CULTURAL CONNECTIONS
Folktale from India

Decide for Yourself

FROM Jataka Tales
EDITED BY NANCY DeROIN

It is said that the Jataka Tales come from Gautama Buddha, who lived in India between 563 and 483 B.C. The stories were passed orally from one generation to the next until they were written down several years after the death of Buddha.

Once upon a time when Brahmadatta was king of Benares, a jackal named Mayavi and his mate lived by the river bank. By this same river, lived two otters, one named Gambhi and one named Anuti.

One day, the two otters were standing on the river bank looking for fish to catch. Gambhi spotted a great rohita fish; he dove into the water after it and grabbed it by the tail. But the fish was so strong that it swam away, dragging the otter behind.

Gambhi called out, "Friend Anuti, help me! I caught this fish, but he's swimming away with me. He's big enough for both of us to eat. Come help!"

Anuti jumped into the river to help his friend.

The two otters dragged the rohita fish out of the water and laid it on the bank. Said Gambhi to Anuti, "How shall we divide it?"

Said Anuti to Gambhi, "I don't know. *You* divide it."

Gambhi protested, "I don't know where to begin. Why don't *you* divide it?" So the otters just stood there on the river bank, unable to decide who should divide the fish or even how to divide it. They soon were overheard by the jackal, Mayavi. He walked toward them with great dignity.

Seeing the jackal, the two otters saluted him respectfully and said:

"Oh, honored sir, we cannot decide how to divide this fish we caught. Can you solve the problem for us?"

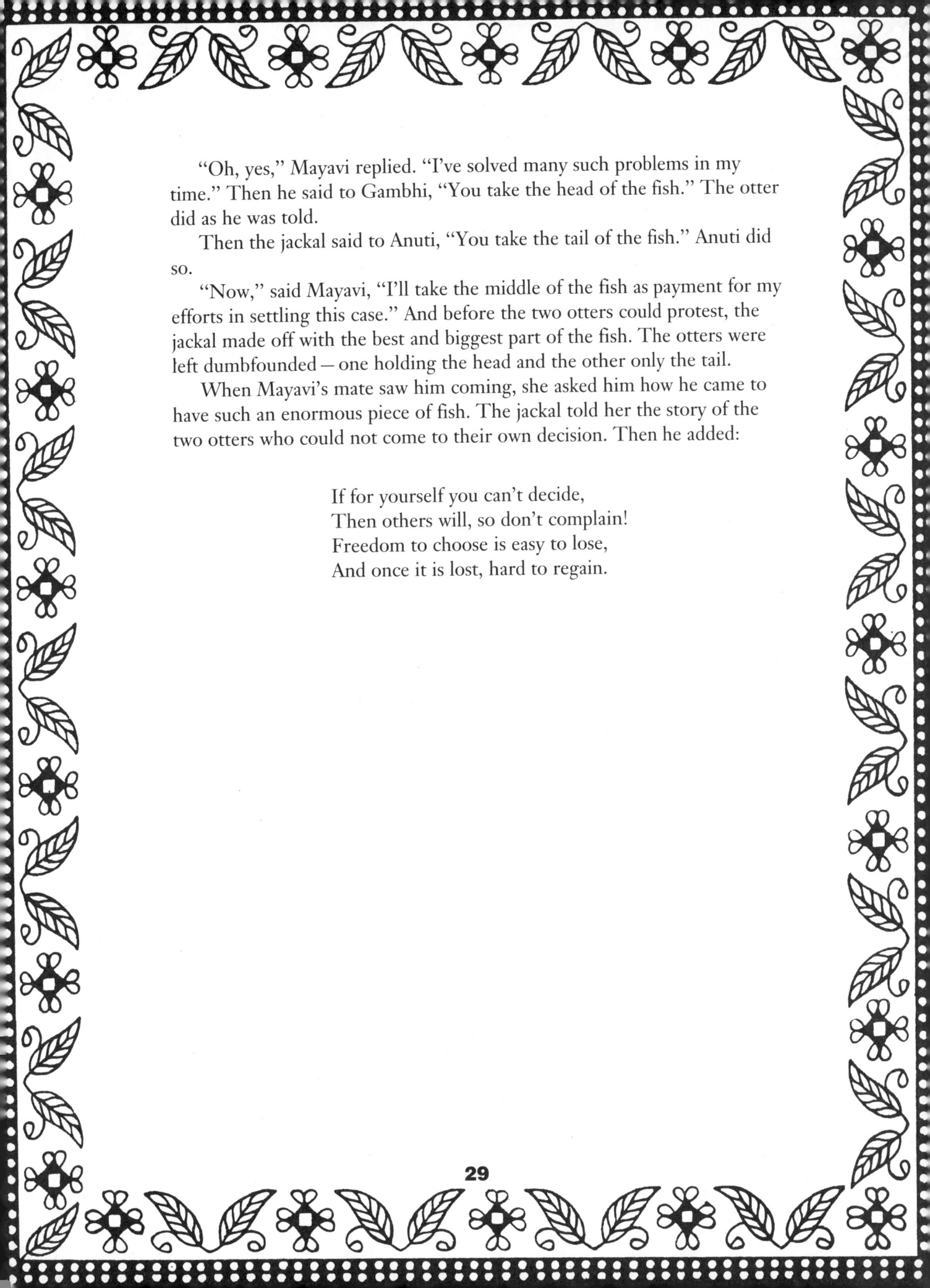

"Oh, yes," Mayavi replied. "I've solved many such problems in my time." Then he said to Gambhi, "You take the head of the fish." The otter did as he was told.

Then the jackal said to Anuti, "You take the tail of the fish." Anuti did so.

"Now," said Mayavi, "I'll take the middle of the fish as payment for my efforts in settling this case." And before the two otters could protest, the jackal made off with the best and biggest part of the fish. The otters were left dumbfounded — one holding the head and the other only the tail.

When Mayavi's mate saw him coming, she asked him how he came to have such an enormous piece of fish. The jackal told her the story of the two otters who could not come to their own decision. Then he added:

> If for yourself you can't decide,
> Then others will, so don't complain!
> Freedom to choose is easy to lose,
> And once it is lost, hard to regain.

Use with Chapter 6, Lesson 9

MATH CONNECTIONS
Money
Multiplication

Ode to Los Raspados

BY GARY SOTO

This poem from Neighborhood Odes *chronicles life in the California neighborhood where Gary Soto grew up. He is also the author of collections of short stories and essays.*

Papá says
They were
A shiny dime
When he was
Little, but for me,
His daughter
With hair that swings
Like jump ropes,
They're free:
Papá drives a truck
Of *helados* and
Snow cones, the
Music of arrival
Playing block
After block.
It's summer now.
The sun is bright
As a hot dime.
You need five
Shiny ones
For a snow cone:

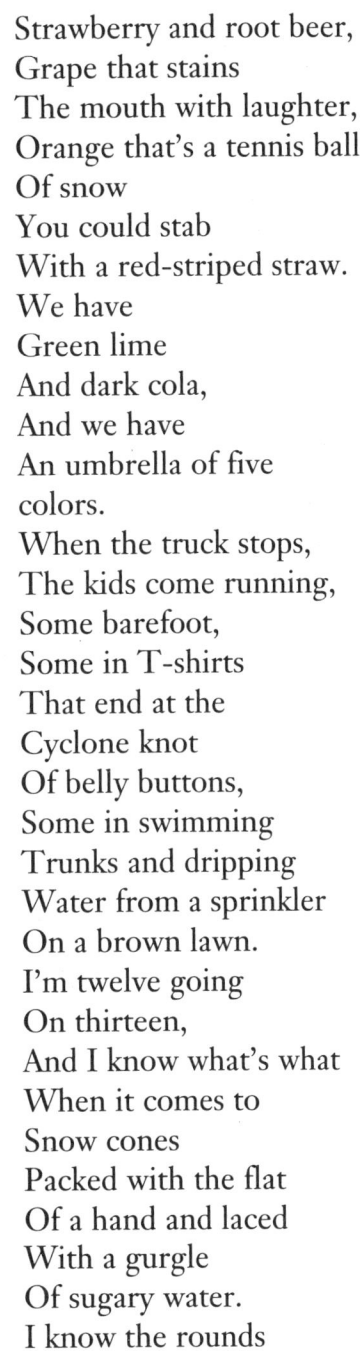

Strawberry and root beer,
Grape that stains
The mouth with laughter,
Orange that's a tennis ball
Of snow
You could stab
With a red-striped straw.
We have
Green lime
And dark cola,
And we have
An umbrella of five
colors.
When the truck stops,
The kids come running,
Some barefoot,
Some in T-shirts
That end at the
Cyclone knot
Of belly buttons,
Some in swimming
Trunks and dripping
Water from a sprinkler
On a brown lawn.
I'm twelve going
On thirteen,
And I know what's what
When it comes to
Snow cones
Packed with the flat
Of a hand and laced
With a gurgle
Of sugary water.
I know the rounds
Of the neighborhood.

I know the kids,
Gina and Ofélia,
Juan and Ananda,
Shorty and Sleepy,
All running
With dimes pressed
To their palms,
Salted from play
Or mowing the lawn.
When they walk away,
The dime of sun
Pays them back
With laughter
And the juice runs
To their elbows,
Sticky summer rain
That sweetens the street.

Use with Chapter 6, Lesson 10

MATH CONNECTIONS

Multiplication
Measurement
Number Patterns

CULTURAL CONNECTION

Folktale from India

The King's Chessboard

BY DAVID BIRCH

All a wise man requires in payment for a service to the king is a grain of rice . . . a grain of rice, that is, on the first square of a chessboard and double that amount on the succeeding squares. A simple enough request until it's carried out!

Once, long ago, in what is now India, there lived a wise man who performed a service for the king of Deccan. In due course the King summoned the wise man to appear before him.

"You have served me well," said the King to the wise man. "What do you wish as a reward?"

The wise man bowed and said, "Serving Your Majesty is reward in itself."

"Indeed, indeed," said the King, "but it must not be said that the King does not reward those who serve him."

"Truly, sire," said the wise man, "I wish no other reward than to serve you again."

"But *I* wish you to be rewarded," said the King in a stern voice. There was a quiet murmuring among the councillors and nobles assembled in the great hall. The King was getting angry. But the wise man seemed not to notice.

"Truly, sire," the wise man said calmly, "I can think of no way you could reward me — "

"You *shall* choose a reward," said the King, "or I promise, you will wish you had!"

The wise man was silent for a long time. And then the small wooden chessboard next to the King seemed to catch his interest.

"Very well, sire," the wise man said at last. "I ask only this: Tomorrow, for the first square of your chessboard, give me one grain of rice; the next day, for the second square, two grains of rice; the next day after that, four grains of rice; then, the following day, eight grains for the next square of your chessboard. Thus for each square give me twice the number of grains of the square before it, and so on for every square of the chessboard."

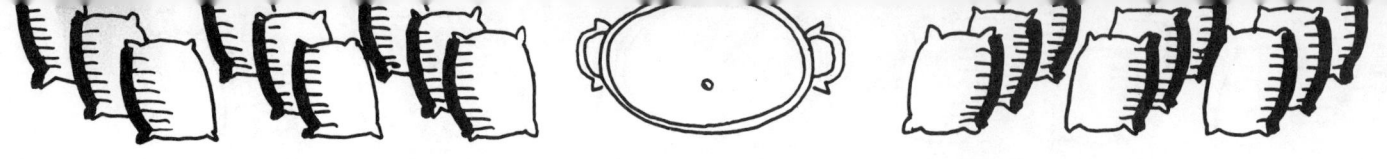

Now the King wondered, as anyone would, just how many grains of rice this would be. He thought of grains of rice on a chessboard: one, two, four, eight, sixteen . . . . There were sixty-four squares. Would that be a pound of rice in all? The King wasn't sure.

At this point the Queen whispered to him, "It seems that the simplest thing to do would be to ask him how much rice that is."

Indeed, that would have been simple; but it would also have made it obvious to everyone that the King was not sure how much rice it was, and the King was too proud to let anyone think he was ever unsure of anything. So he did not ask the question. Instead, he smiled royally and said to the wise man, "Your complicated request is most simply granted."

This caused a stirring of laughter among the councillors and nobles, and as the wise man bowed and quietly left the hall, there was much amusement at this simple old man and his odd request.

To add to the humor the Grand Superintendent of the King's Granaries had a servant, wearing the most splendid garments, carry the first little grain of rice on a gleaming silver tray to the wise man's house. But the wise man merely thanked the servant and placed the grain on the first square of his chessboard.

When the King heard this, he placed a grain of rice on the first square of his own chessboard.

On the second day two grains of rice were sent to the wise man, and the King and the wise man each placed a grain of rice on the second square of his chessboard. And so it went: four grains of rice to the wise man on the third day and a grain of rice on the third square, and so on.

On the eighth day there was no servant in splendid dress, but only an ordinary granary worker bringing one hundred twenty-eight grains of rice in a small pouch. The wise man placed one grain on the eighth square of his chessboard and threw the rest to a bird outside his window. By now the King had quite forgotten the wise man and his rice, and it was left to a servant to place a grain on the eighth square of the King's chessboard.

The actual counting of the grains of rice was left to the Weigher of the King's Grain: two hundred fifty-six grains, then five hundred twelve, then one thousand twenty-four.

"Dear me," said the Weigher to himself on the twelfth day, "soon I'll be counting grains all day long." So instead of counting out two thousand forty-eight grains of rice, he simply weighed out an ounce of rice and sent it to the wise man.

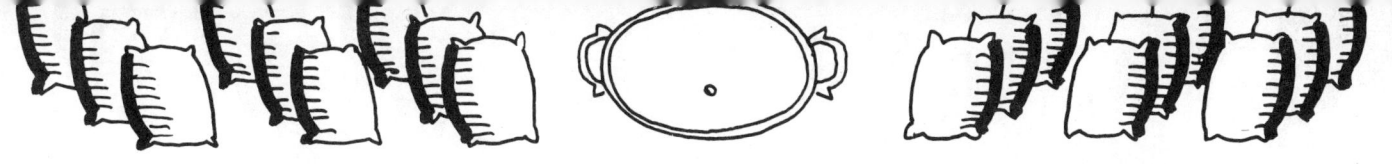

Only four days later the wise man was sent a small bag of rice weighing sixteen ounces, or one pound. He placed one grain on the sixteenth square of his chessboard and gave the rest to a beggar.

But at the granaries the Weigher had become worried.

"Tomorrow," he said to himself, "it will be two one-pound bags, and the next day it will be four." He calculated the amounts: eight, sixteen, thirty-two . . . . When he got to two-thousand forty-eight bags, he stopped in alarm. "I must tell the Grand Superintendent of the King's Granaries at once!"

But when he was actually standing before the Grand Superintendent, the Weigher became so nervous that he didn't say what he meant to say.

"Your — Your Excellency," he stammered, "excuse me . . . the rice sent to the wise man is . . . excuse me . . . How many small bags of rice are there in the King's granaries?"

"What kind of question is that?" demanded the Grand Superintendent. "Weigher, have you been drinking?

"N-no, Your Excellency," the Weigher said. Then he hurried back to his scales and promised himself not to bother anybody again about the wise man's rice.

It was only nine days later that the Grand Superintendent saw four granary workers carrying sacks of rice from the granary. Following them was a group of ragged children.

"Here! Stop!" shouted the Grand Superintendent. "Where are you going with the King's rice?"

When the children laughed at this, the Grand Superintendent demanded, "And why are these urchins so merry?"

"Your Excellency," said one of the granary workers, "we are carrying this rice to the wise man, who then gives it away to the poor and hungry."

"Impossible!" said the Grand Superintendent. "That fool of a Weigher has made some mistake."

But there had been no mistake.

It was explained how one grain became two and then four; grains became ounces; ounces became pounds; a bag became two bags; and today it was four sacks, each weighing one hundred twenty-eight pounds.

The Grand Superintendent said to himself, "Tomorrow there will be eight sacks — over half a ton! I must tell the King!"

But the King was away hunting in the mountains that day and the next. So on the following day the Grand Superintendent had to send the wise man over a ton of rice. The next day it was two tons. And still the King had not returned to the palace. There was nothing to be done . . . . The next day four tons . . . . Then eight tons.

On the day after that, when the King returned, he heard a great cheering outside his palace. From his window he saw sixteen wagons, each carrying sixteen sacks of rice — over a ton on each wagon. The wagons were followed by a crowd of happy people.

"Where are those wagons going?" the King demanded.

"Sire," said the Grand Superintendent of the King's Granaries, "That is the rice being sent today to the wise man."

"Impossible!" said the King. "You have made some mistake!"

"I fear not, sire," said the Grand Superintendent, and began to explain how one grain became two, then one ounce became two ounces, then a pound became —

"Enough!" said the King. "Summon the royal mathematicians."

The mathematicians appeared and were ordered to determine how many tons of rice the King had in fact promised to the wise man. After an hour of calculating and recalculating, the Chief Mathematician rather nervously held up a slate with their answer.

As the King read the number he grew angrier and angrier. "Five hundred forty-nine billion, seven hundred fifty-five million, eight hundred thirty thousand, eight hundred eighty-seven tons!"

"Tons!" roared the King. "Tons! Deception and treason!" He then ordered everyone from his presence except the Queen.

He sat and glared at his chessboard with its thirty-one grains of rice — thirty-one days since he insisted the wise man should be rewarded. After a time the Queen said to him, "You must ask the wise man to release you from your promise. It is the only thing to be done."

But the King seemed not to hear.

Finally the Queen left him alone with his anger and silence. There he sat all that day and there he stayed all that night, dozing fitfully until he was awakened by the first light of morning.

Below he saw a line of thirty-two wagons leaving the granaries and huge, happy crowds following them.

The King sighed. He placed a grain of rice on the thirty-second square of his chessboard and then gave orders to summon the wise man to the palace.

"This must stop," said the King to the wise man. "There is not enough rice in all of India to reward you."

"No, indeed, sire," said the wise man. "There is not enough rice in all the world."

"Then," said the King, "since I have promised you the impossible, I command you as my loyal subject to tell me how you will be satisfied."

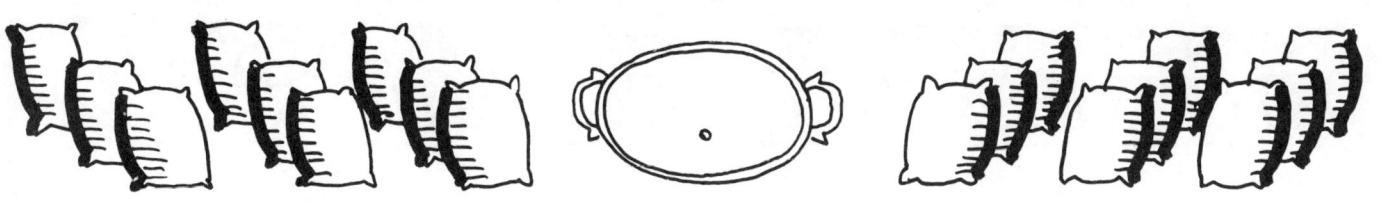

"But I *am* satisfied, sire," said the wise man. "It is as I tried to tell you, sire. I have always been satisfied. It was *you* who insisted on rewarding me. It is *you* who must be satisfied."

As the wise man spoke these words all the splendid people in the great hall became very, very still.

"*Are* you satisfied, sire?" asked the wise man. And although he spoke quietly, everyone heard him as if he had shouted. No one whispered. No one moved.

"Yes," said the King at last. "Yes, I am satisfied."

Then he smiled at the wise man, not a happy smile perhaps, but a genuine smile. "And I understand," the King said, "that in all this you have done me yet another service."

"Then, sire, I am truly rewarded," said the wise man. With that he bowed very low and left the great hall.

The wise man returned to his simple home and quiet life. And although he was to serve the King many times afterward, the question of a reward never again arose.

The King ruled wisely and justly for many, many years, and to the end of his days he kept the chessboard with its thirty-two grains of rice to remind him of the wise man's lesson — how easy it is for pride to make a fool of anyone, even a king.

Use with Chapter 7, Lesson 1

MATH CONNECTIONS
Division
Fractions

CULTURAL CONNECTION
Folktale from Ethiopia

The Divided Students

FROM The Rich Man and the Singer
TOLD BY MESFIN HABTE-MARIAM

Four hungry students learn an important lesson about sharing when they find a piece of bread. This folktale is tied into the opener for this chapter.

Four students were walking home when suddenly they saw a big piece of bread lying in the road.

They all ran to pick it up. They bumped into each other and rolled on the ground, grabbing at the bread. Each of them tried to get it for himself. They struggled and argued fiercely.

One of them tried to settle the dispute by telling the others he was the oldest. He would take charge of the bread and divide it equally among them all. But the others refused to listen and went on arguing.

Presently a priest passed by and asked them what was the trouble. They told him, and of course each student claimed to have found the bread first.

The priest said, "Give the bread to me. I will divide it into four pieces and give you your fair shares."

The students agreed. The priest took the bread and divided it into four parts. Then he put the pieces of bread in a row and showed each student his share. They stretched out their hands to take the bread, but the priest stopped them.

"Oh, no," said he. "Wait until I am sure that all the pieces are exactly equal in size."

"You are right, Father," said one of the students. "My share is the smallest."

"Of course," said the priest, "your share is indeed the smallest. But this one is the biggest." And he ate a mouthful of the biggest piece of bread.

"Do not worry, my children, all your shares will soon be equal. Now here is one that is still too big!" And he took another piece and ate almost half of it.

"Alas!" cried one of the students. "That was my piece and it was the right size. Why do you take half of it?"

"Do not worry, my child," said the priest. "I will make the others equal to yours." And he ate a mouthful of each of the other three pieces.

But still they were not equal.

"Just a bite here and a bite there, and all will be well!" said he.

The students watched him in bewildered silence until the priest swallowed the last mouthful of bread and left them standing in the road.

They looked into each other's eyes, and at last the oldest student said: "I told you I would divide the bread fairly among us. You would not listen to me. Therefore we have lost everything we had."

They remembered the words of the old saying: "United we stand; divided we fall." And they went sadly on their way with equal shares — of nothing at all.

Use with Chapter 8, Lesson 4

MATH CONNECTION
Geometry
CULTURAL CONNECTIONS
Folktale from China

Grandfather Tang's Story

**BY ANN TOMPERT
ILLUSTRATED BY ROBERT ANDREW PARKER**

After reading the story and looking at the illustrations, students will enjoy using tangrams to create their own stories.

Grandfather Tang and Little Soo were sitting under a peach tree in their backyard. They were amusing each other by making different shapes with their tangram puzzles.

"Let's do a story about the fox fairies," said Little Soo. So Grandfather Tang arranged his seven tangram pieces into the shape of a fox.

Then Grandfather Tang made another fox with Little Soo's seven tangram pieces. Little Soo clapped her hands as her grandfather began.

40

Although Chou and Wu Ling were best friends, they were always trying to outdo each other. One day this rivalry almost brought their friendship to a tragic end. They were sitting under their favorite willow tree beside a river talking about their magic powers.

"I can change myself into a rabbit as quick as a wink," boasted Wu Ling. "I'll bet you can't do that."

"I can too," said Chou.

"Can not," said Wu Ling. "Anyway, actions speak louder than words." And he changed himself into a

rabbit.

"Not bad," said Chou, smoothing his whiskers. "But watch me do better than that."

And before Wu Ling could blink, Chou changed from a fox into a

dog!

Now, when Chou changed himself into a dog, he not only looked like a dog, but he felt like a dog and acted like a dog. He bared his teeth and lashed his tail. Wu Ling shivered and twitched his nose.

"I love rabbits," Chou growled," and I'm going to get you and gobble you up."

The dog edged closer and closer. Wu Ling's eyes grew bigger and bigger. He was too frightened to move at first. But then he thought, "I'll be safe if I can climb up the willow tree."

His little puff of a tail grew long and bushy and his tall ears shrunk as Wu Ling transformed himself into a

squirrel.

Wu Ling sprang into the willow tree and scrambled to the top.

"Chou will probably turn himself into a cat so he can climb up the tree after me," Wu Ling said to himself. "But he'll never catch me. I'll jump from tree to tree, and he won't be able to follow me."

Of course, Chou thought about changing himself into a cat.

"But that's just what Wu Ling expects me to do," he said to himself. "What can I do to surprise him?"

He thought and thought.

"I know. I'll swoop down upon him from above."

And he turned himself into a

hawk.

Chou circled round and round in the sky above the willow tree, searching for Wu Ling. Wu Ling peered through the leaves of the tree, looking for Chou on the ground.

Round and round Chou circled the willow tree until he spied Wu Ling.

"*Kek! Kek! Kek!*" he shrieked as he zoomed down upon the squirrel.

Wu Ling trembled. Chou's beak looked sharp enough to pierce right through him.

"If only I lived in a shell house," he thought. "Then Chou couldn't hurt me."

Chou stuck out his fierce claws to seize Wu Ling, but Wu Ling dove toward the river below the willow tree. And as he dove he tucked in his head and tail and legs, turned green, and changed into a

turtle.

Wu Ling climbed up on a mossy rock in the middle of the river. He thought he was safe because he looked as if he were a part of the rock. Chou circled round and round, searching and searching, until his sharp eyes spotted the turtle. Then he swooped down, down, down toward him.

But just as Chou reached him, Wu Ling plunged into the water.
"Follow me and you'll drown," he cried.
"Don't worry," cried Chou, plunging right behind Wu Ling.

His body grew longer, covered with scales. He whipped the water with his long, wicked tail. And he snapped his spike-toothed jaws as he turned into a

crocodile.

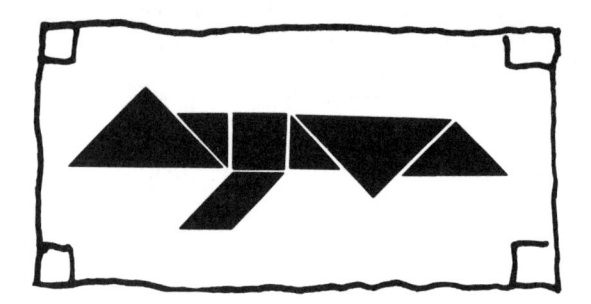

Wu Ling circled round and round as he plunged down, down, down to the bottom of the river. Chou lashed his wicked tail as he plunged after Wu Ling. Just as they reached the bottom, Chou clamped Wu Ling in his spike-toothed mouth.

"Now, I've got you!" he bellowed through his clenched teeth.

"Oh, no, you haven't," cried Wu Ling, who grew smaller and smaller and changed himself from green to gold as he transformed himself into a

goldfish.

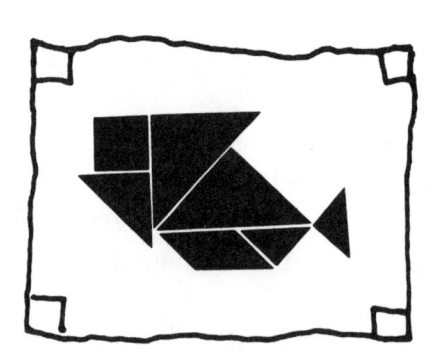

And he swam out of Chou's mouth between his spiked teeth.

Then he hid in a patch of cattails. Chou churned the water with his lashing tail as he charged into the patch after Wu Ling. With his head swinging back and forth and his eyes darting here and there, he searched for Wu Ling. Wu Ling knew that Chou would not give up until he found him.

"I must fly from here," he thought.

And he started to honk as he transformed himself into a

goose.

"*Honk! Honk! Honk!*" called Wu Ling.

And he took to the air.

A chorus of honks swelled the air as the flock of geese spread their wings to follow him. While Chou watched, the honking grew fainter, the flock grew smaller, and he felt his anger slowly drain away.

"Why, oh, why did we play that stupid game?" he moaned. "I'll never see Wu Ling again."

He closed his eyes and sank toward the river's bottom. Just as he touched it, however, he had an idea. And up he popped again, a goose himself.

Chou charged after him, but Wu Ling spread his wings and took to the air.

Chou watched him fly to a small island where a flock of geese were feeding. By now he was not only very angry, he was also very hungry. He decided that if he could not catch Wu Ling, any goose would make him a good dinner. He splashed through the water toward the island until he reached it.

Moments later, Chou was flying after Wu Ling and the other geese. He could hardly see or hear them at first. But he did not let this discourage him. Calling upon every last bit of his strength, he forged ahead.

Each flap of his wings brought him closer. The wedge of geese slowly grew bigger. The honking grew louder. At last Chou found himself flying beside Wu Ling.

"I'm tired of our silly game," he cried. "Come back with me to our willow tree."

Before Wu Ling could answer, something stung Chou's right wing. He sank toward the ground.

A hunter had shot him. Wu Ling flew down beside Chou, placed his left wing under Chou's smashed right wing, and together they fluttered down to the edge of the forest.

The hunter ran toward them.

"Fly away," Chou urged Wu Ling. "Save yourself. Fly! Fly!"

"I won't desert you," cried Wu Ling.

And with a mighty roar, he changed into a

lion.

The hunter raised his bow. Wu Ling sprang toward him and knocked the bow from his hand. The hunter fled, leaving his bow behind.

Wu Ling and Chou returned to their fox shapes. And Wu Ling helped Chou to his den, where he took care of him until he was mended.

Did they ever play that game again?" asked Little Soo.

"Many times," said her grandfather. "But they were very, very careful."

"That was a good story," said Little Soo. "Let's do another."

Grandfather arranged his seven tangram pieces.

"Is this story going to be about a man?" asked Little Soo.

"Yes," said her grandfather. "He's old and he's tired. He wants to sit under a tree and rest awhile."

"Is he a grandfather like you?" asked Little Soo.

"Yes," said her grandfather. "Just like me."

Little Soo arranged the seven pieces of her tangram beside her grandfather's.

"Is that a little girl?" he asked.

"Yes," said Little Soo. "Just like me. She'll sit and rest beside the man."

"That will make him very happy," said Grandfather Tang. "And now, Little Soo, what will we do?"

"We'll sit and rest together until Mother calls us for supper," said Little Soo.

"That will make me very happy," said her grandfather.

Use with Chapter 9, Lesson 11

MATH CONNECTION
Measurement
CULTURAL CONNECTION
Folktale from England and North America

Telling the Horses Apart

FROM Noodles, Nitwits, and Numskulls
BY MARIA LEACH

Two foolish men who cannot tell their horses apart decide to measure the animals. They find that there is indeed a difference in size — the white horse is taller than the black one! Your students may enjoy creating their own stories using measurement.

Once there were two fools who used to go horseback riding together, but they never could tell their horses apart.

So one of them docked his horse's tail. That was fine: now one had a long tail and one had a short tail. The fools could tell them apart.

Then one day the long-tailed horse got his tail caught in a gate, and after that the two tails were the same length.

So one fool put a notch in his horse's ear. Now one horse had a notched ear and the other didn't, and it was easy to tell the horses apart.

Then one day the other horse notched his ear on a wire fence, and after that their ears were alike.

Finally the two fools thought of measuring the horses! And they discovered that the white horse was two inches taller than the black horse. After that they had no trouble.

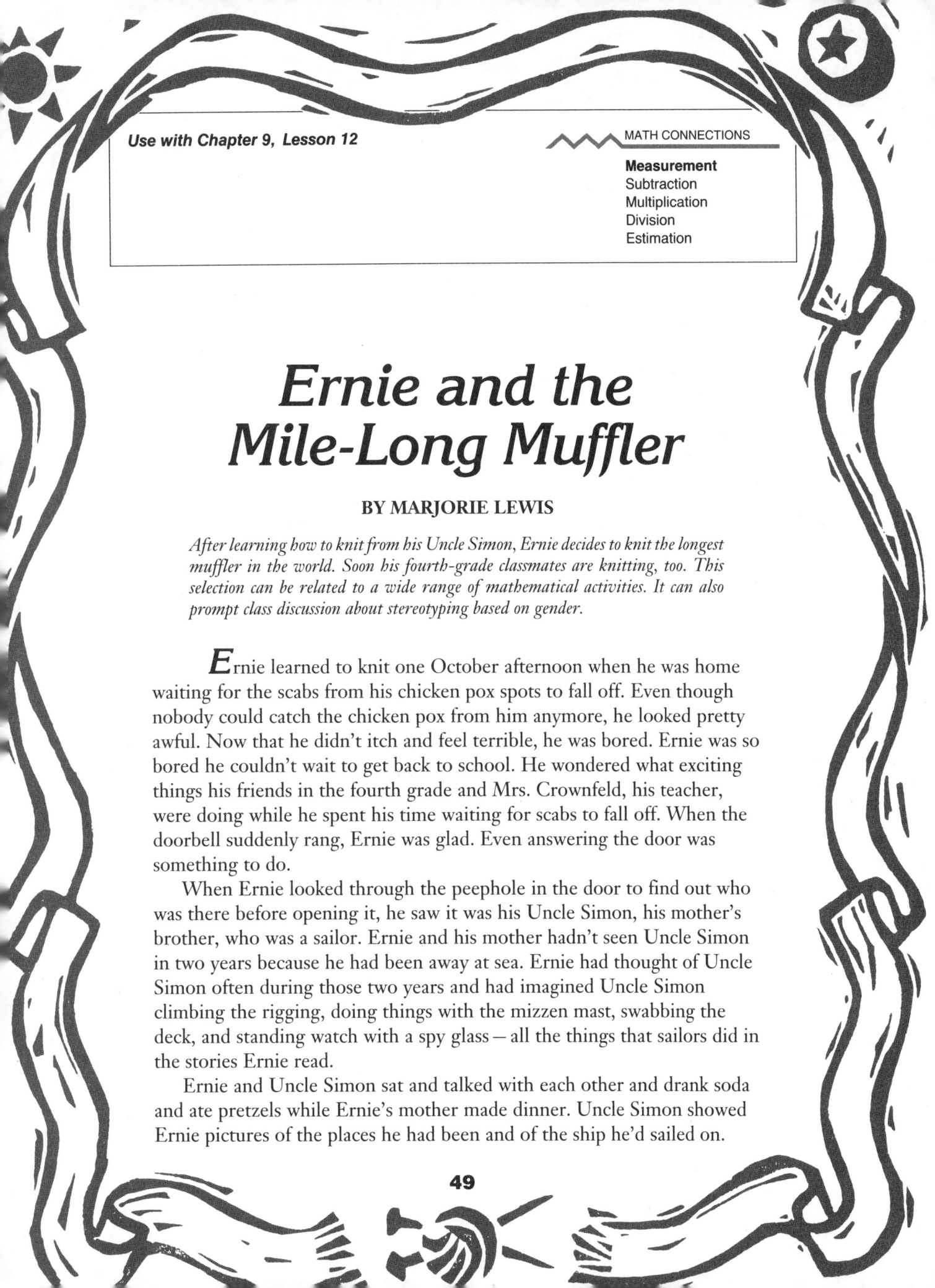

Use with Chapter 9, Lesson 12

MATH CONNECTIONS

Measurement
Subtraction
Multiplication
Division
Estimation

Ernie and the Mile-Long Muffler

BY MARJORIE LEWIS

After learning how to knit from his Uncle Simon, Ernie decides to knit the longest muffler in the world. Soon his fourth-grade classmates are knitting, too. This selection can be related to a wide range of mathematical activities. It can also prompt class discussion about stereotyping based on gender.

  *E*rnie learned to knit one October afternoon when he was home waiting for the scabs from his chicken pox spots to fall off. Even though nobody could catch the chicken pox from him anymore, he looked pretty awful. Now that he didn't itch and feel terrible, he was bored. Ernie was so bored he couldn't wait to get back to school. He wondered what exciting things his friends in the fourth grade and Mrs. Crownfeld, his teacher, were doing while he spent his time waiting for scabs to fall off. When the doorbell suddenly rang, Ernie was glad. Even answering the door was something to do.

  When Ernie looked through the peephole in the door to find out who was there before opening it, he saw it was his Uncle Simon, his mother's brother, who was a sailor. Ernie and his mother hadn't seen Uncle Simon in two years because he had been away at sea. Ernie had thought of Uncle Simon often during those two years and had imagined Uncle Simon climbing the rigging, doing things with the mizzen mast, swabbing the deck, and standing watch with a spy glass—all the things that sailors did in the stories Ernie read.

  Ernie and Uncle Simon sat and talked with each other and drank soda and ate pretzels while Ernie's mother made dinner. Uncle Simon showed Ernie pictures of the places he had been and of the ship he'd sailed on.

Then Uncle Simon asked Ernie what he liked best to eat. Ernie told him his best thing was a hamburger with red onion circles, lots of ketchup on the top part, lots of mayonnaise on the bottom part, and a roll with seeds to hold it all together. Ernie told Uncle Simon his worst thing to eat was anything shaky. Uncle Simon said he didn't like shaky things either, especially tapioca pudding because the tapioca beads look like fish eyes. Uncle Simon told Ernie all about the weird foods he had eaten in his travels: rattlesnake, turtle soup, candied grasshoppers, rabbit stew, cows' eyes, calves' brains, chocolate-covered ants. Ernie began to feel sick.

Uncle Simon changed the subject and asked Ernie what kinds of things he liked to do. Ernie told him about reading comics and cereal boxes, trading baseball cards, making cookies, and shooting baskets.

Uncle Simon told Ernie he liked most to read mystery stories; next, to bake bread; and third, to knit. He told Ernie that on his ship, when he wasn't working, he had lots of time to do all three. Ernie said that he didn't know that men knitted. Uncle Simon said that men have knitted for centuries, especially men in armies and navies who spend a lot of time waiting for things to happen. Uncle Simon opened his sea bag and took out a sweater that looked like a rainbow and let Ernie try it on. Ernie thought it was the most terrific sweater he had ever seen. Then Uncle Simon took some knitting needles out of his bag and a big ball of yellow yarn. By the time Ernie's mother called them for dinner, Uncle Simon had taught Ernie to knit.

The next few days, while Ernie waited for the scabs to fall off and his spots to fade, he knitted a sweater for his dog Buster, socks for his father's golf clubs, a Christmas stocking for the canary, and a muffler for his mother for her birthday. The muffler was so beautiful and fit his mother's neck so well that Ernie decided to make mufflers for everyone he knew. Then he had a better idea. The idea came to him one morning while he was eating breakfast and reading his world-record book for the hundred-millionth time. Ernie decided that he would knit the world's longest muffler. He would make it a mile long! Ernie wrote a letter to Uncle Simon, who was back at sea, and told him about his plan.

He asked his mother to get all the record books she could find in the library. Ernie looked through all of them and found that none of them mentioned a record for muffler-knitting. Ernie pictured himself holding the victorious knitting needles crossed in front of him with foot after foot of muffler looping around the throne he would be sitting on when they took his picture for the record book.

Ernie told his mother about his idea. She told him that there were 5,280 feet in a mile. Then Ernie and his mother figured out that there were 63,360 inches in a mile. Ernie's mother said that it would sure be a lot of muffler to knit!

Ernie asked his mother to ask her friends to give him all the extra yarn they had. By the time Ernie was well enough to go back to school, he had finished about two feet of muffler. Ernie thought that the two feet had been done so quickly that it wouldn't be hard at all to do a mile of knitting.

His first day back at school, Ernie packed his gym bag with his gym shorts, his T-shirt, and his knitting. He kept his knitting with him all morning. When he was sitting and waiting for late-comers to be present for morning attendance, or for the assembly program to begin, or for the fire drill to be over, Ernie knitted. Mrs. Crownfeld said she thought it was wonderful to be able to knit and asked Ernie if, after recess, he would demonstrate to the class how to knit. Ernie said he would.

At recess, the class went outside. Ernie sat down on the bench to wait for his turn to shoot baskets. He took out his knitting.

"I can't believe you're doing that," said Frankie.

"I mean my *mother* does that!" said Alfred.

"So what," said Ernie. "Your mother bakes cookies, Alfred, and so do you. And so do I."

"It's different," Alfred said. "Knitting is different."

Alfred watched while Ernie's fingers made the needles form stitches. When Edward came over, Frankie and Alfred moved away. Edward leaned over and watched Ernie.

"No boy I ever saw did that," Edward said. "Boys don't do that." Edward reached out and grabbed the ball of yarn tearing it off from the knitting. Ernie watched silently while Edward, Frankie, and Alfred played basketball with the yarn ball. Then they dropped it into a puddle. They fished it out and tossed it to Ernie.

Ernie looked at the ball of yarn with glops of mud and leaves tangled in it. Then he put his needles and the two feet of muffler on the bench and threw it away into the bushes.

The three boys, Frankie, Alfred, and Edward formed a circle around Ernie. They began to run around like crazies with their thumbs in their ears and their fingers flapping yelling: "Nyah, nyah, Ernie knits!" Over and over again. Then the three boys called Ernie a nitwit (or was it a knitwit? thought Ernie miserably). The other children in the class came over to watch. Some of them joined the group around Ernie.

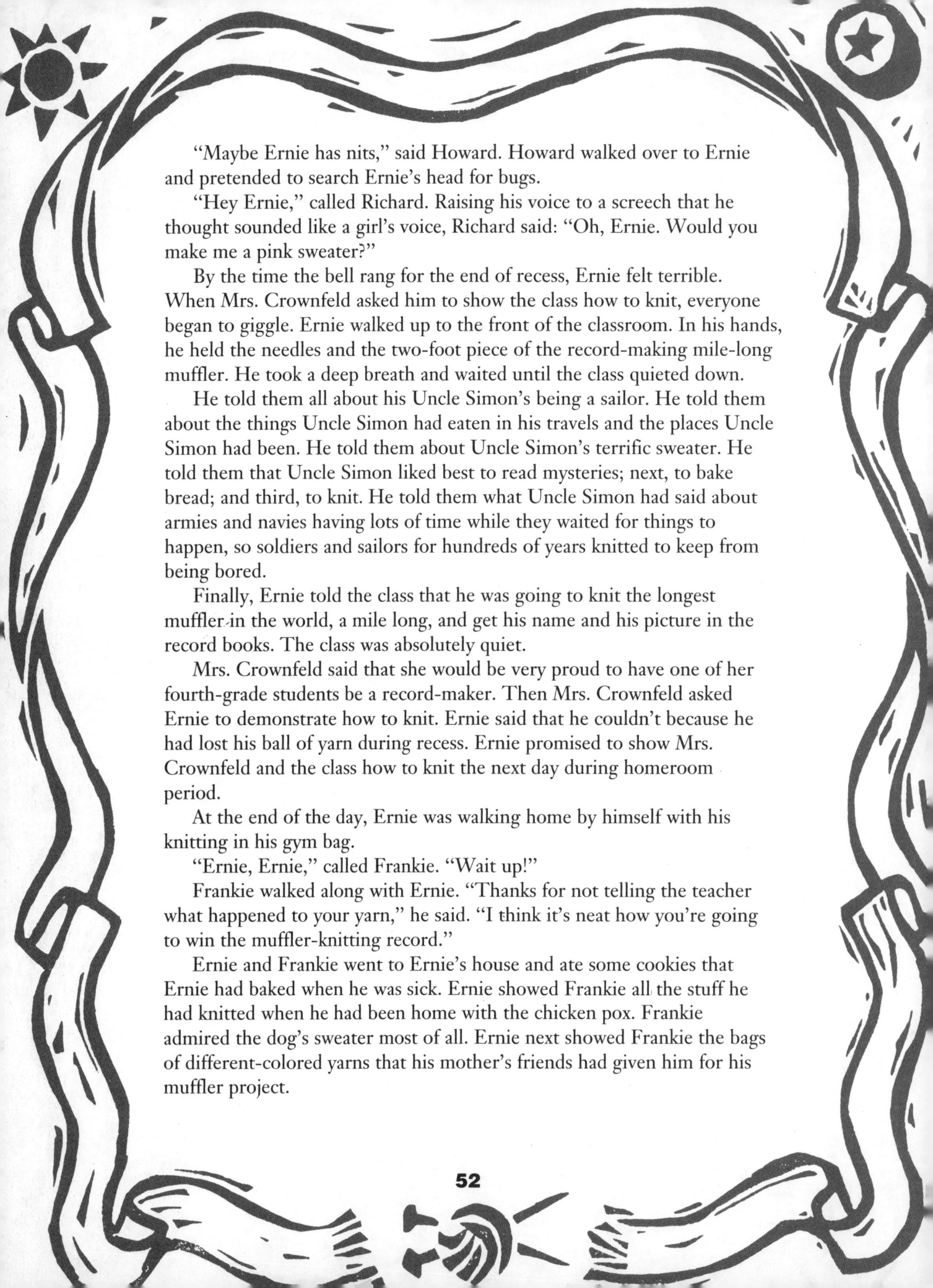

"Maybe Ernie has nits," said Howard. Howard walked over to Ernie and pretended to search Ernie's head for bugs.

"Hey Ernie," called Richard. Raising his voice to a screech that he thought sounded like a girl's voice, Richard said: "Oh, Ernie. Would you make me a pink sweater?"

By the time the bell rang for the end of recess, Ernie felt terrible. When Mrs. Crownfeld asked him to show the class how to knit, everyone began to giggle. Ernie walked up to the front of the classroom. In his hands, he held the needles and the two-foot piece of the record-making mile-long muffler. He took a deep breath and waited until the class quieted down.

He told them all about his Uncle Simon's being a sailor. He told them about the things Uncle Simon had eaten in his travels and the places Uncle Simon had been. He told them about Uncle Simon's terrific sweater. He told them that Uncle Simon liked best to read mysteries; next, to bake bread; and third, to knit. He told them what Uncle Simon had said about armies and navies having lots of time while they waited for things to happen, so soldiers and sailors for hundreds of years knitted to keep from being bored.

Finally, Ernie told the class that he was going to knit the longest muffler in the world, a mile long, and get his name and his picture in the record books. The class was absolutely quiet.

Mrs. Crownfeld said that she would be very proud to have one of her fourth-grade students be a record-maker. Then Mrs. Crownfeld asked Ernie to demonstrate how to knit. Ernie said that he couldn't because he had lost his ball of yarn during recess. Ernie promised to show Mrs. Crownfeld and the class how to knit the next day during homeroom period.

At the end of the day, Ernie was walking home by himself with his knitting in his gym bag.

"Ernie, Ernie," called Frankie. "Wait up!"

Frankie walked along with Ernie. "Thanks for not telling the teacher what happened to your yarn," he said. "I think it's neat how you're going to win the muffler-knitting record."

Ernie and Frankie went to Ernie's house and ate some cookies that Ernie had baked when he was sick. Ernie showed Frankie all the stuff he had knitted when he had been home with the chicken pox. Frankie admired the dog's sweater most of all. Ernie next showed Frankie the bags of different-colored yarns that his mother's friends had given him for his muffler project.

"Say, Ernie," said Frankie. "I bet my mother's got some yarn left over from the sweater she knitted for my sister. I'll ask her if I can give it to you."

"That would be great, Frankie," said Ernie. "I'm going to need all the yarn I can get!"

The next day in school, Ernie showed the class how the needles went in front of the stitch to make a knit stitch and how it went in the back to make a purl stitch. He showed them how the two kinds of stitches together made the bumpy ridges that kept the sleeves tight at the wrists. He showed the class how to make the pieces get bigger and smaller to fit next to each other so that they could be sewn together to make a swell outfit. He offered to teach anyone in class who wanted to learn. Mrs. Crownfeld was the first to ask Ernie for lessons.

Gradually, everyone in fourth grade learned to knit. Mrs. Crownfeld made a deal with them: the class could knit during homeroom, firedrills (while they were outside waiting to go back in), or rainy-day recess, plus a special knitting time right after lunch each day when the class could knit while Mrs. Crownfeld put her knitting aside and read them a story from the library.

In return for all the knitting lessons from Ernie, the class brought in all the yarn they could get from anyone who would give it to them. Ernie kept the yarn in a plastic garbage bag in the corner of the classroom. Each day, a knitting monitor measured Ernie's muffler and wrote the measurement in a diary book Mrs. Crownfeld had given the class as a present.

By Thanksgiving, Ernie's muffler was sixteen feet long and Ernie was looking pale. He never went outside to play anymore. He didn't do anything at all but go to school, do his homework, eat his meals, and knit. Cynthia, who was very good in math, subtracted the sixteen feet Ernie had finished from the 5,280 feet in a mile. That left 5,264 feet to go before the end of school. Since school would be over and summer vacation begin in twenty-eight weeks, Ernie would have to knit over 188 feet of muffler *every week*, or about 27 feet *every day* (including Saturday and Sunday) to finish the muffler by the end of fourth grade.

Ernie listened to Cynthia very carefully. He remembered the picture he had dreamed of: sitting on a throne, his knitting needles crossed in front of him, foot after foot of muffler looping around him. His name and photograph in the record books. The pride in the faces of his mother and his teacher. The admiration of all his friends. Then Ernie thought of how long it had been since he played with his friends or baked cookies or read a book — or even a cereal box.

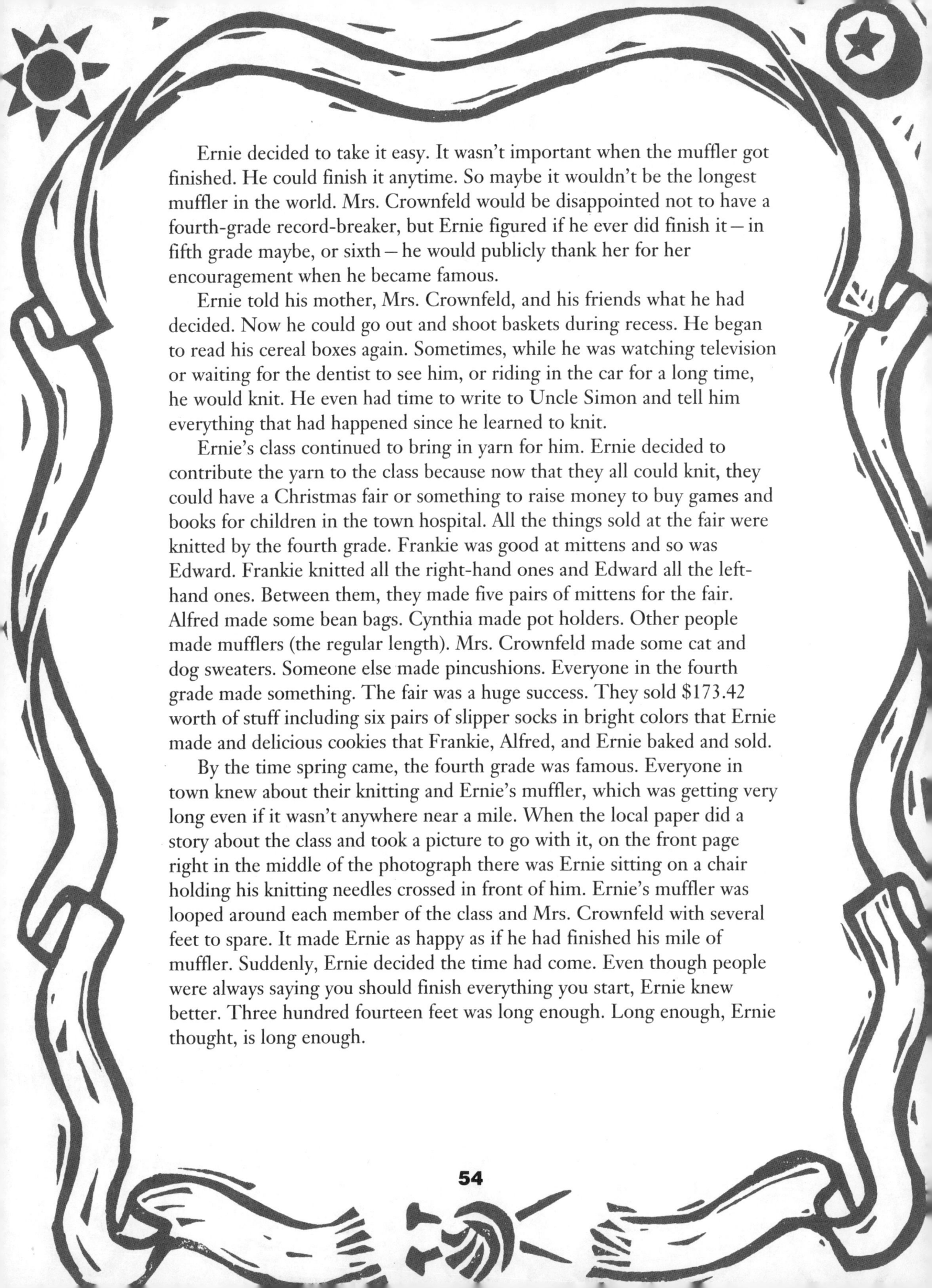

Ernie decided to take it easy. It wasn't important when the muffler got finished. He could finish it anytime. So maybe it wouldn't be the longest muffler in the world. Mrs. Crownfeld would be disappointed not to have a fourth-grade record-breaker, but Ernie figured if he ever did finish it — in fifth grade maybe, or sixth — he would publicly thank her for her encouragement when he became famous.

Ernie told his mother, Mrs. Crownfeld, and his friends what he had decided. Now he could go out and shoot baskets during recess. He began to read his cereal boxes again. Sometimes, while he was watching television or waiting for the dentist to see him, or riding in the car for a long time, he would knit. He even had time to write to Uncle Simon and tell him everything that had happened since he learned to knit.

Ernie's class continued to bring in yarn for him. Ernie decided to contribute the yarn to the class because now that they all could knit, they could have a Christmas fair or something to raise money to buy games and books for children in the town hospital. All the things sold at the fair were knitted by the fourth grade. Frankie was good at mittens and so was Edward. Frankie knitted all the right-hand ones and Edward all the left-hand ones. Between them, they made five pairs of mittens for the fair. Alfred made some bean bags. Cynthia made pot holders. Other people made mufflers (the regular length). Mrs. Crownfeld made some cat and dog sweaters. Someone else made pincushions. Everyone in the fourth grade made something. The fair was a huge success. They sold $173.42 worth of stuff including six pairs of slipper socks in bright colors that Ernie made and delicious cookies that Frankie, Alfred, and Ernie baked and sold.

By the time spring came, the fourth grade was famous. Everyone in town knew about their knitting and Ernie's muffler, which was getting very long even if it wasn't anywhere near a mile. When the local paper did a story about the class and took a picture to go with it, on the front page right in the middle of the photograph there was Ernie sitting on a chair holding his knitting needles crossed in front of him. Ernie's muffler was looped around each member of the class and Mrs. Crownfeld with several feet to spare. It made Ernie as happy as if he had finished his mile of muffler. Suddenly, Ernie decided the time had come. Even though people were always saying you should finish everything you start, Ernie knew better. Three hundred fourteen feet was long enough. Long enough, Ernie thought, is long enough.

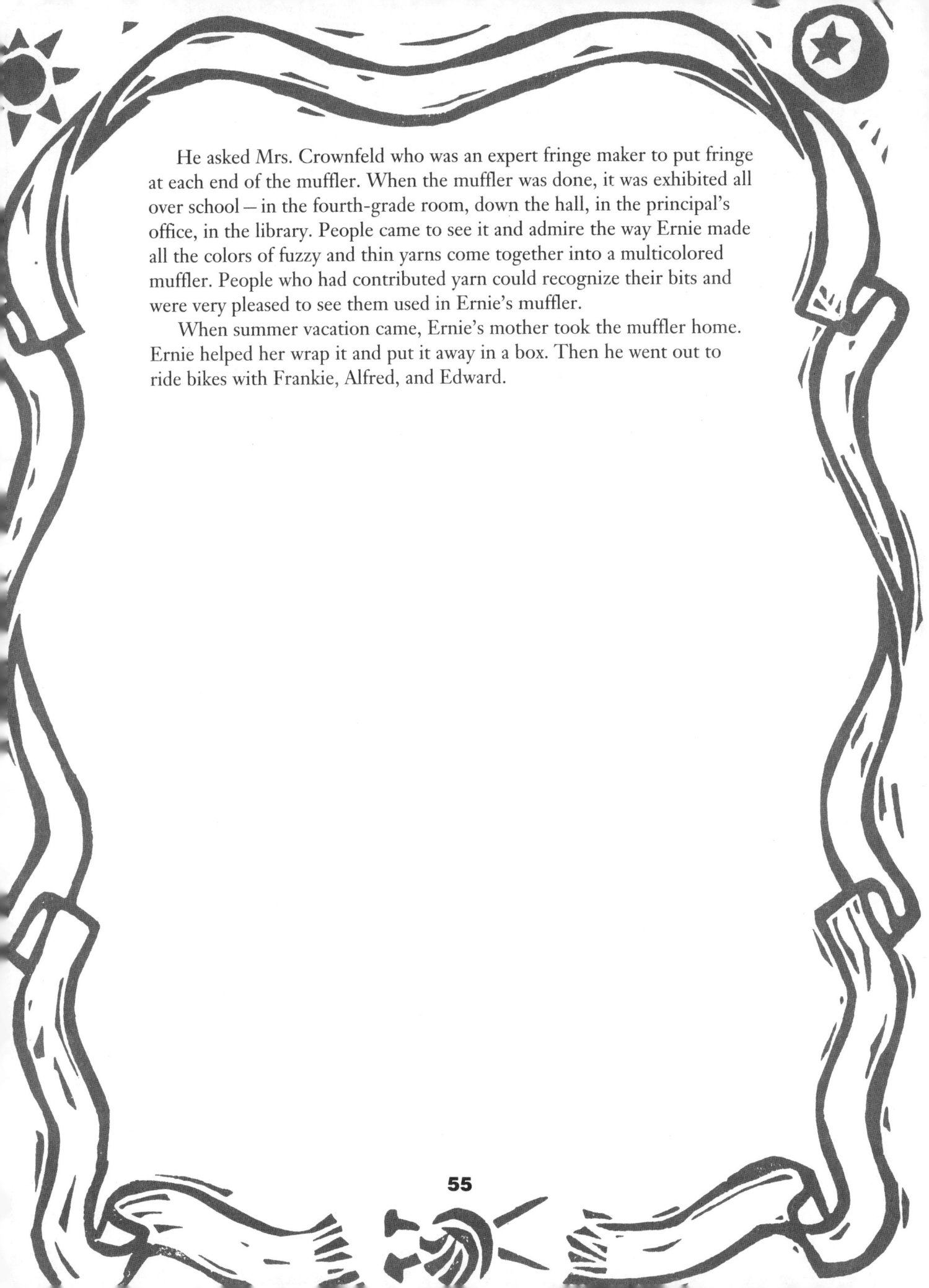

He asked Mrs. Crownfeld who was an expert fringe maker to put fringe at each end of the muffler. When the muffler was done, it was exhibited all over school — in the fourth-grade room, down the hall, in the principal's office, in the library. People came to see it and admire the way Ernie made all the colors of fuzzy and thin yarns come together into a multicolored muffler. People who had contributed yarn could recognize their bits and were very pleased to see them used in Ernie's muffler.

When summer vacation came, Ernie's mother took the muffler home. Ernie helped her wrap it and put it away in a box. Then he went out to ride bikes with Frankie, Alfred, and Edward.

Use with Chapter 10, Lesson 12

MATH CONNECTION
Measurement
CULTURAL CONNECTION
Folktale from Turkey

Lightening the Load

FROM Noodles, Nitwits, and Numskulls
BY MARIA LEACH

The man from Gotham is kindhearted, but the animal he is riding probably wishes he had less heart and more brain. You may wish to explain to students that an ass is a long-eared mammal of the horse family, such as a donkey.

Another man of Gotham, kindhearted fellow, was riding home one day from a mill where he had bought a big sack of meal. He rode with the sack flung before him across the ass's back.

After a while in the heat of the day, he thought the poor ass must be exhausted with the weight of the load. So he lifted up the sack and laid it across his own shoulders.

"That will lighten the load," he said.

Use with Chapter 11, Lesson 3

MATH CONNECTION
Decimals

Math Class

BY MYRA COHN LIVINGSTON

In addition to using this poem with the activity suggested, you may wish to have students talk about the times when their attention starts drifting and how they can refocus it.

She talks about the decimal point,
The reasons why—
But on the window, buzzing free,
A fly

With two red eyes
Moves slowly up the pane.
She moves the decimal one place left
And then again

The fly moves up
And up, practiced and slow.
What I have learned of decimal points
Flies know.

Use with Chapter 12, Lesson 2

MATH CONNECTIONS

Estimation
Multiplication
Number Patterns

Multiplication

This poem gives students the opportunity to exercise both mental math and estimation skills. You may also wish to suggest the students use a calculator to check their estimates.

One times one is one,
And now I've got that done.

Two times one is two —
I know, and so do you.

Three times one is three —
That's very plain to see.

But fifty-nine times eight
Is hard to calculate.

And sixty-eight times ninety-seven,
I may not learn 'til I'm eleven!

Unknown

INDEX

•INDEX BY TITLE•

Decide for Yourself, 28
Divided Students, The, 38
Don't Make a Bargain With a Fox, 25

Ernie and the Mile-Long Muffler, 49

Farmer and the Merchant, The, 13
Following a Formula, 7

Good Hotdogs, 3
Grandfather Tang's Story, 40

How the Terrapin Beat the Rabbit, 8

Jinxed or Not?, 5

King's Chessboard, The, 33

Lightening the Load, 56

Math Class, 57
Multiplication, 58

Ode to Los Raspados, 30

Pocket Calculator, 15

Race that was Rigged, The, 10

Setting a Limit, 2

Telling the Horses Apart, 48

Wesley Paul, Marathon Runner, 20
Wonderful Wooden Clock, The, 16

•INDEX OF MATH CONNECTIONS•

ADDITION

Farmer and the Merchant, The, 13
Good Hotdogs, 3
How the Terrapin Beat the Rabbit, 8
Pocket Calculator, 15
Wesley Paul, Marathon Runner, 20

DECIMALS

Math Class, 57

DIVISION

Decide for Yourself, 28
Divided Students, The, 38
Don't Make a Bargain With a Fox, 25
Ernie and the Mile-Long Muffler, 49
Farmer and the Merchant, The, 13
Good Hotdogs, 3

ESTIMATION

Ernie and the Mile-Long Muffler, 49
Multiplication, 58

FRACTIONS

Decide for Yourself, 28
Divided Students, The, 38
Don't Make a Bargain With a Fox, 25

GEOMETRY

Grandfather Tang's Story, 40

MEASUREMENT

Ernie and the Mile-Long Muffler, 49

King's Chessboard, The, 33
Lightening the Load, 56
Race that was Rigged, The, 10
Telling the Horses Apart, 48
Wesley Paul, Marathon Runner, 20

MONEY

Farmer and the Merchant, The, 13
Good Hotdogs, 3
Ode to Los Raspados, 30

MULTIPLICATION

Ernie and the Mile-Long Muffler, 49
Farmer and the Merchant, The, 13
Good Hotdogs, 3
King's Chessboard, The, 33
Multiplication, 58
Ode to Los Raspados, 30

NUMBER PATTERNS

King's Chessboard, The, 33
Multiplication, 58

NUMBER SENSE

Following a Formula, 7
How the Terrapin Beat the Rabbit, 8
Jinxed or Not?, 5
Pocket Calculator, 15
Setting a Limit, 2

STATISTICS

Following a Formula, 7

SUBTRACTION

Ernie and the Mile-Long Muffler, 49
Farmer and the Merchant, The, 13
Good Hotdogs, 3
How the Terrapin Beat the Rabbit, 8
Pocket Calculator, 15
Wesley Paul, Marathon Runner, 20

TIME

Wonderful Wooden Clock, The, 16
Wesley Paul, Marathon Runner, 20

•INDEX BY CATEGORY•

STORIES

Decide for Yourself, 28
Divided Students, The, 38
Don't Make a Bargain With a Fox, 25

Ernie and the Mile-Long Muffler, 49

Farmer and the Merchant, The, 13
Following a Formula, 7

Grandfather Tang's Story, 40

How the Terrapin Beat the Rabbit, 8

Jinxed or Not?, 5

King's Chessboard, The, 33

Lightening the Load, 56

Race that was Rigged, The, 10

Setting a Limit, 2

Telling the Horses Apart, 48

Wesley Paul, Marathon Runner, 20
Wonderful Wooden Clock, The, 16

POEMS

Good Hotdogs, 3

Math Class, 57
Multiplication, 58

Ode to Los Raspados, 30

Pocket Calculator, 15

•INDEX BY AUTHOR•

Birch, David, 33

Cisneros, Sandra, 3

DeRoin, Nancy, 28

Fogel, Julianna A., 20

Greaves, Nick, 10

Habte-Mariam, Mesfin, 13, 38

Jagendorf, M. A., and R. S. Boggs, 25

Katz, Bobbi, 15

Leach, Maria, 48, 56
Lewis, Marjorie, 49
Livingston, Myra Cohn, 57

Patterson, Lillie, 16

Scheer, George F., 8
Soto, Gary, 30
Sullivan, George, 2, 5, 7

Tompert, Ann, 40

•INDEX OF SELECTIONS BY CONTINENT•

AFRICA

Race that was Rigged, The, 10
By Nick Greaves

Ethiopia

Divided Students, The, 38
By Mesfin Habte-Mariam

Farmer and the Merchant, The, 13
By Mesfin Habte-Mariam

ASIA

China

Grandfather Tang's Story, 40
By Ann Tompert

India

Decide for Yourself, 28
Retold by Nancy DeRoin

King's Chessboard, The, 33
By David Birch

Turkey

Lightening the Load, 56
Retold by Maria Leach

EUROPE

England

Telling the Horses Apart, 48
Retold by Maria Leach

Turkey

Lightening the Load, 56
Retold by Maria Leach

NORTH AMERICA

African American

Wonderful Wooden Clock, The, 16
By Lillie Patterson

Native American

How the Terrapin Beat the Rabbit, 8 (*Cherokee*)
Edited by George F. Scheer

North American Contemporary

Decide for Yourself, 28
Retold by Nancy DeRoin

Divided Students, The, 38
Told by Mesfin Habte-Mariam

Don't Make a Bargain With a Fox, 25
By M. A. Jagendorf and R. S. Boggs

Ernie and the Mile-Long Muffler, 49
By Marjorie Lewis

Farmer and the Merchant, The, 13
Told by Mesfin Habte-Mariam

Following a Formula, 7
By George Sullivan

Good Hotdogs, 3
By Sandra Cisneros

Grandfather Tang's Story, 40
By Ann Tompert

How the Terrapin Beat the Rabbit, 8
Edited by George F. Scheer

Jinxed or Not?, 5
By George Sullivan

King's Chessboard, The, 33
By David Birch

Math Class, 57
By Myra Cohn Livingston

Multiplication, 58

Ode to Los Raspados, 30
By Gary Soto

Pocket Calculator, 15
By Bobbi Katz

Race that was Rigged, The, 10
Told by Nick Greaves

Setting a Limit, 2
By George Sullivan

Wesley Paul, Marathon Runner, 20
By Julianna A. Fogel

Wonderful Wooden Clock, The, 16
By Lillie Patterson

North American Traditional

Lightening the Load, 56
Retold by Maria Leach

Telling the Horses Apart, 48
Retold by Maria Leach

SOUTH AMERICA

Argentina

Don't Make a Bargain With a Fox, 25
Retold by M. A. Jagendorf and R. S. Boggs

ACKNOWLEDGMENTS *(continued)*

GRANDFATHER TANG'S STORY by Ann Tompert, illustrated by Robert Andrew Parker. Text copyright © 1990 by Ann Tompert. Reprinted by permission of Ann Tompert and her agent, Kirchoff/Wohlberg. Illustrations copyright © 1990 by Robert Andrew Parker. Tangrams reprinted by permission of Crown Publishers, Inc.

"Ode to Los Raspados" from NEIGHBORHOOD ODES by Gary Soto. Copyright © 1992 by Gary Soto. Reprinted by permission of Harcourt Brace Jovanovich, Inc.

"The Wonderful Wooden Clock" from BENJAMIN BANNEKER: GENIUS OF EARLY AMERICA by Lillie Patterson. Copyright © 1978 by Lillie Patterson. Reprinted by permission of the author.

"How the Terrapin Beat the Rabbit" from CHEROKEE ANIMAL TALES edited by George F. Scheer. Copyright © 1968 by George F. Scheer. Reprinted by permission of George F. Scheer.